LANZI'S

HISTORY OF PAINTING

IN

UPPER AND LOWER ITALY.

TRANSLATED AND ABRIDGED

BY

THE REV. G. W. D. EVANS, A.M.

IN TWO VOLUMES.

VOL. II.

LONDON:
J. HATCHARD AND SON, 187, PICCADILLY.

1831.

LONDON:
IBOTSON AND PALMER, PRINTERS, SAVOY STREET, STRAND.

CONTENTS

TO

THE SECOND VOLUME.

NEAPOLITAN SCHOOL.

CHAPTER I.

CHAPTER II.

CHAPTER III.

CHAPTER IV.

VENETIAN SCHOOL.

CHAPTER V.

CHAPTER VI.

CHAPTER VII.

CHAPTER VIII.

MANTUAN SCHOOL.

CHAPTER IX.

CHAPTER X.

MODENESE SCHOOL.

CHAPTER XI.

CHAPTER XII.

CHAPTER XIII.

PARMESAN SCHOOL.

CHAPTER XIV.

CHAPTER XV.

CREMONESE SCHOOL.

CHAPTER XVI.

CHAPTER XVII.

CHAPTER XVIII.

MILANESE SCHOOL.

CHAPTER XIX.

CHAPTER XX.

CHAPTER XXI.

BOLOGNESE SCHOOL.

CHAPTER XXII.

CHAPTER XXIII.

CHAPTER XXIV.

ERRATUM.

Page 58, line 15, *for* Cesare de Cesto, *read* Cesare da Sesto.

LANZI'S HISTORY OF PAINTING

ABRIDGED.

NEAPOLITAN SCHOOL.

EPOCH I.

THE OLD MASTERS.

Dominici, and other Neapolitan biographers, affirm that Naples was not destitute of painters even during the dark ages. In proof of which they adduce various sacred pieces by anonymous artists, of a date considerably anterior to 1200; particularly a good many Madonnas in the old style, the objects of veneration in the churches where they are placed.

The first painter, after the revival of art, whose name is recorded, is Tommaso de' Stefani, who flourished in the time of Cimabue, and during the reign of Charles of Anjou. According to Vasari, this prince was, on his way through Florence, taken to Cimabue's studio, to see the picture which he had painted for the Rucellai chapel; containing a figure of the Virgin, the largest that had ever been executed till then. Dominici has not failed to turn this to the advantage of his countryman Tommaso. He observes that King Charles would have invited Cimabue to Naples, had he considered him an accomplished painter: Charles, however, did no such thing; but, on the contrary, employed Tommaso to decorate one or two churches that he had founded: consequently, the latter must have appeared to him superior to Cimabue. Every one must see that such reasoning as this cannot determine the relative merit of the two painters: this must be decided by their existing works; and judging from these, Marco da Siena, the father of the history of painting as regards the Neapolitan school, gave it as his opinion, that in grandeur of style Cimabue had the advantage. The Minutoli chapel, at the cathedral, mentioned by Boccaccio, was by Tommaso embellished with various pieces on the subject of the Crucifixion.

About the year 1325, Giotto was invited to Naples by King Robert, for the purpose of painting in the church of S. Chiara; as he accordingly did, executing various pieces from the Gospel history and the mysteries of the Apocalypse, from hints previously suggested to him by Dante, as the story went in Vasari's time. These pictures, in consequence of their rendering the church too dark, were whitewashed over about the commencement of the present (eighteenth) century: some of the best figures, however, were suffered to remain in their pristine state, as was also a figure of the Virgin, styled the Madonna della Grazia, which the piety of the distinguished nuns to whom it belonged, preserved for the veneration of the faithful. Giotto had for his companion in his labours one Maestro Simone, who, in consequence of the esteem in which he was held by Giotto, acquired a high reputation at Naples. Dominici more especially commends a Descent from the Cross, painted on panel for the larger altar of the church della Incoronata; comparing it even to Giotto's performances. For the rest, he acknowledges that Simone never attained to equal merit in conception or invention, and never succeeded in imparting the same graceful air to his heads, or the same sweetness to his colouring.

He initiated in the art a son of his, called Francesco di Simone, of whom there is, in the church of S. Chiara, a chiaroscuro representing the Virgin, which has been much commended,—a figure which was also spared during the whitewashing above recorded. Gennaro di Cola and Stefanone were also disciples of his; they resembled each other closely in style, and hence were colleagues in the execution of some large works. The former was, for the time in which he lived, a pains-taking and correct painter; one who was solicitous to overcome the difficulties of art, and promote its advancement; whence he sometimes betrays a degree of constraint: the latter displays greater genius, and greater boldness of colouring; imparting to his figures a vivacity which might have raised him to eminence, had he lived at a more auspicious period.

Till Zingaro introduced at Naples a style borrowed from various other schools, the art was but at a low ebb in that city and its dependencies. Of this Francesco's scholar Colantonio del Fiore, who lived till the year 1444, affords sufficient proof; for Dominici, on mentioning certain pictures which pass for his, expresses a doubt whether they are not rather the work of Maestro Simone; which is a kind of tacit acknowledgment that, during the course of a century, the art had made but little progress. He had a scholar named Angiolo Franco, who imitated Giotto's manner better than any other of the Neapolitans; adding to it, however, a stronger chiaroscuro, which he derived from his master.

Antonio Solario, (originally a blacksmith,) commonly called *Lo Zingaro*, contributed more than the last-mentioned painter to the advancement of art. Solario's story has in it something of the romantic; for being enamoured of a daughter of Colantonio's, and being told by the latter that he would give him his daughter after the lapse of ten years, provided he became by that time a good painter, Solario exchanged the forge for the studio, and substituted the pencil for the file. From Naples he betook himself to Bologna, where he was for several years the scholar of Lippo Dalmasio, styled also, from the number of Madonnas he painted, and the grace with which he represented them, Lippo dalle Madonne. Quitting Bologna, he travelled through the greater part of Italy, for the purpose of familiarising himself with the style of other schools. In his heads he displayed great merit, insomuch that he extorted the admiration even of Marco da Siena, who used to say that "they looked as though they were alive." Considering, too, the time at which he lived, he also distinguished himself by his perspective, and the judicious composition of his pieces; which he contrived to diversify with landscapes better than did others, as well as to embellish with dresses peculiar to the age and accurately imitated. In the drawing of his hands and feet he was less happy; and was sometimes guilty of extravagance of gesture and crudeness of colouring. Having returned to Naples, and given a specimen of his accomplishments, and being, as the story goes, recognized and admired by Colantonio, he became his son-in-law, nine years from the time of his having quitted that city; where, during the reign of Alphonso, he both cultivated the art himself, and gave lessons in it till 1455, about which period he died.

Meanwhile there started up at Naples a new school; which, from its most original and most celebrated prototype, was styled by the Cav. Massimo the school of Zingaro; and the pictures executed from Zingaro's time down to the days of Tesauro, or thereabouts, are at Naples usually denominated *Zingaresche*, just as those which were executed in imitation of Berrettini are every where denominated *Cortonesche*.*

* The most distinguished of the *Zingareschi* were Pietro and Polito del Donzello, and Silvestro Buoni; and the most eminent scholar of this latter was, Bernardo Tesauro, who approached the modern manner more closely than any of his predecessors.

NEAPOLITAN SCHOOL.

EPOCH II.

AT NAPLES THE MODERN STYLE OWES ITS ORIGIN TO THE FOLLOWERS OF RAFFAEL AND MICHAEL ANGELO.

It has already been observed that, after the commencement of the sixteenth century, the art of painting appeared to be every where matured, and every where began to put on a peculiar character which served to distinguish school from school. The Neapolitan has not been able to boast such marks of originality as certain others of the Italian schools; but it has afforded scope for the introduction of the best methods, according as youthful artists on quitting their native place happen to have carried thither the style of this or that particular master; and according as the Neapolitan sovereigns and nobles happen to have invited, or at least employed, the most distinguished foreign painters,—a point in which, with the exception of Rome, Naples yields not perhaps to any city of Italy. This city, which is equally rich in palaces and churches, has always possessed a number of eminent artists worthy to undertake its decoration. Nor has it ever been deficient in men of genius; the natives being prolific of those who are capable of prosecuting any study with success; especially such as demand a warm imagination, and a sort of animating fire. Hence one who was at the same time distinguished for his attainments both in literature and the arts, declared, that no other part of Italy could boast so many who may be said to have been born painters; such is the fervour, the fertility of fancy, and the boldness visible in the greater part of their works. To this fervid temperament also, may we refer that rapidity of execution on which both ancients and moderns have lavished their encomiums, when it happens not to be divorced from other meritorious qualities. But for the most part, it precludes accuracy of design; which accordingly must not be looked for in many of the artists of this school. Neither must we expect to find much predilection for the *beau idéal*: the greater part, as is usual with those who copy from nature, having borrowed the features of their countenances and the action of their figures from the populace; some with more, some with less carefulness of selection. With regard to colouring, this school has changed its maxims with change of times. In point of invention and composition, it may be reckoned among the most copious; but cannot be ranked among the most studied.

At Naples, the era of modern painting could not have commenced under more auspicious cir-

circumstances than those which fell to its lot. Pietro Perugino had painted an Assumption of the Virgin at the cathedral, which, as I am informed, is still in being. This work served to pave the way for the improved taste. Raphael and his school now coming into repute, Naples was the first among foreign cities to profit by the circumstance, owing to some of the disciples of that school; to whom were added, towards the middle of the century, some of the followers of Michael Angelo. Hence, down to about the year 1600, this school looked up to none except to these two consummate masters, and their imitators; save that some few also copied after Titian.

Andrea Sabbatini of Salerno, who became enamoured of Pietro's style from the moment he beheld that picture of his at the cathedral, set out, at the very first opportunity, for Perugia, with a view to attend his school. In consequence, however, of what fell from certain painters, with whom he met at some inn on the road, and who had seen the works executed by Raphael for Julius II., he changed his purpose; and repairing to Rome, put himself under the care of that great master. With Raphael, however, he remained but a short time; the death of his father compelling him, against his will, to return to Salerno in 1513; but he returned quite another man. It is said that he wrought in company with Raphael at the church della Pace and at the Vatican, and that he became a good copyist of his figures: certain it is that he imitated his style with success. Compared with his fellow-students, he does not soar so high as Giulio Romano, yet he surpasses Raphael del Colle and others of a similar stamp; displaying a skilfulness of design, a selection in his proportions and attitudes, together with a predilection for chiaroscuro, a tendency to prominence of muscle, a fulness of drapery, and a colouring which still retains its freshness after the lapse of so many years. He executed a good many works at Naples, as well as at his native place, at Gaeta, and throughout almost the whole of the kingdom, for the ornament of churches and private collections; where we meet with Madonnas of his of the highest beauty.*

* Sabbatini's scholars were Cesare Turco, Francesco and Fabrizio Santafede, and Pistillo. In the year 1527, Polidoro da Caravaggio went to Naples, where he formed some scholars, among them, Giambernardo Lama, Francesco Ruviale, and Marco Cardisco. Shortly after Polidoro, Gianfrancesco Penni (il Fattore) also visited Naples; his followers there were Il Pistoia, Francesco Curia, and Ippolito Borghese. Perino del Vaga had also some scholars among the Neapolitan artists, as Gio. Corso, and Gianfilippo Criscuolo; from whose school proceeded Francesco Imparato, the father of Girolamo Imparato, also a distinguished artist. Vasari was invited to Naples in 1544, and Marco da Siena visited it about 1558, where he formed various pupils.

NEAPOLITAN SCHOOL.

EPOCH III.

CORENZIO, RIBERA, CARACCIOLO, FORM THE CABAL AT NAPLES. STRANGERS WHO COMPETE WITH THEM.

About the middle of the sixteenth century, Tintoretto, of the Venetian school, began to be ranked among the more distinguished painters; while toward the close of the same century Caravaggio, of the Roman, and the Caracci, of the Lombard school, also rose to the highest eminence. The three several styles of these masters soon spread over the rest of Italy, and in Naples became the predominant ones, being adopted there by three artists of considerable note, Corenzio, Ribera, and Caracciolo. These men, who came into notice one after another, afterwards formed a coalition for the exclusion of other painters and the mutual advancement of themselves. During the period that these three were in the greatest repute, Guido, Domenichino, Lanfranco, and Artemisia Gentileschi, spent some time at Naples, and both there and elsewhere contributed some pupils to the Neapolitan school. Thus the period that intervened between Bellisario and Giordano, forms the brightest epoch of this school; if we regard only the number of distinguished artists and the many works of taste which it produced: but if we take into account the unworthy artifices and flagitious deeds to which it gave birth, it is the blackest era to be found not only in the Neapolitan school, but in the whole annals of art.

CORENZIO.

Bellisario Corenzio, a native of Greece, after having spent five years in the school of Tintoretto, settled in Naples about the year 1590. Nature had endowed him with a fertility of imagination and a rapidity of execution, that enabled him almost to equal his master in the prodigious number of his pictures even of the larger size. Four painters, even of the more diligent of the tribe, could hardly have executed so much as he contrived to get through alone. He is not, however, to be compared with Tintoretto, who, when he chose to repress his enthusiasm, is second to few in design; and displays an inventiveness, a movement, and a vivacity in his heads, which the Venetians themselves, with his works constantly before their eyes, have never been able to equal. Nevertheless, Corenzio successfully imitated him when he chose to take pains; as in the great picture painted for the refectory of the Benedictine Fathers, where he represented the miraculous Feeding of the Multitude by our Saviour,—a work completed in forty days. But for the most part he adopted a manner conformable, in many respects, to the style of D'Arpino; in others, partaking of the Venetian school; not, however, without something of a character peculiar to himself, especially in his glories, which he encumbered with dark clouds, apparently surcharged with rain,—a character which, in the judgment of the Cav. Massimo, shows him to have been "rather fertile in invention than studious of the beautiful." He painted but little in oils, though he displayed great merit in the strength and union of his colours. An inordinate thirst of gain led him to undertake large works in fresco, in which he had a ready knack at drawing advantage from expedients, being copious, varied, energetic, and happy in the general effect; nay, even studied and correct in the details, whenever the proximity of some formidable rival compelled him to be so. Such was the case at the Certosa in the chapel of St Januarius. There he tasked his powers to the utmost, being goaded on by the proximity of a work of Caravaggio's, who had embellished that place with an altar-piece, which remained there a long time, admired as one of his most beautiful performances, and which was subsequently removed into the monastery. In other churches may be seen sacred pieces painted by him in small proportions, on which Dominici bestows the highest encomiums.

RIBERA.

To what country Giuseppe Ribera really belonged has been matter of dispute. Palomino, following Sandrart and Orlandi, will have it that he was a native of Spain; in proof of which he adduces a picture of St. Matthew with the following inscription:—"Jusepe de Ribera espagnol de ciutad de Xativa; reyno de Valencia, Accademico romano anno 1630." The Neapolitans affirm that he was born in the neighbourhood of Lecce, but of a Spanish father; and that to recommend himself to the government, which was Spanish, he always boasted of this extraction, and invariably alluded to it in subscribing his name, whence he derived the appellation of Spagnoletto. The controversy has, however, of late years been decided; it having been proved by the evidence of an extract from the baptismal register kept at Sativa (now

San Filippo, that he was there born. (See the *Antologia di Roma* of 1795.) We read that he even acquired the rudiments of the art in Spain from Francesco Ribalta of Valencia, supposed to have been a scholar of Annibal Carracci. But the history of the Neapolitan school, which, in its account of this artist, I now look upon as unsuspicious, affirms on the contrary, that Ribera, while still a youth, or rather, while a mere boy, studied at Naples under Caravaggio, about the year 1606, at the time that master, who had fled from Rome in consequence of a murder he had committed, betook himself thither, where he executed a number of works both for private individuals and for the different churches. But whoever may have been the master from which he derived instruction in his boyish years, it appears certain that Caravaggio was, even in early life, his chosen and favorite model. Subsequently, on seeing the works of Raphael and Annibal Carracci at Rome, and those of Correggio at Modena and Parma, Ribera adopted, after their example, a graver and more pleasing style, in which, however, he persevered only a short time, and with but little success; there being at Naples others who pursued the same path, and whom it was by no means easy to surpass. He returned, therefore, to Caravaggio's manner, which, by its truth, force, and strong chiaroscuro, attracts the multitude more than a gayer style: in a short time he was made painter to the court; and in the sequel became the arbiter of its taste.

The studies he had gone through rendered him superior to Caravaggio in invention, selection, and design; in imitation of whom he executed at the Certosini that grand Descent from the Cross, which, in the opinion of Giordano, was of itself sufficient to form an excellent painter, and might compare with the brightest productions of art. The Martyrdom of St. Januarius in the royal chapel, and the St. Jerome at the church of the Trinità, possess greater beauty than most of his works, and may be said to be somewhat after the manner of Titian. St. Jerome, indeed, was his favourite subject. A great number either of full or half-length figures of this saint are to be met with in different collections: in that of the Panfili palace at Rome we find about five, and all different. Nor are other pictures of his of a similar description rarely to be met with—anchorites, prophets, and apostles—in which he displays a prominence of bone and muscle, and a gravity of countenance, which he copied for the most part from nature. In the same taste are most of his pictures from profane story, in which he delights to represent old men and philosophers; as, for instance, the Democritus and Heraclitus, in the possession of the Marquis Jerome Durazzo,—figures so much in the style of Caravaggio. In choosing historical subjects for the exercise of his pencil, the most revolting were to him the most inviting—murders, executions, barbarous tortures. Of these, one of the most celebrated is the Ixion on the wheel, in the palace of Buen Retiro at Madrid. Ribera's works are very numerous, more especially in Italy and Spain. On this head, however, we must not omit to warn the reader, that, of the many reputed Spagnolettos to be found in different collections, we may not merely suspect, but at once take for granted, that a great proportion are falsely attributed to him, and ought rather to be called the works of his scholars.

CARACCIOLO.

Giambattista Caracciolo, a follower, first of Francesco Imparato, and afterwards of Caravaggio, attained the age of manhood without having produced any work calculated to bring him into notice. Roused afterwards by the fame of Annibale, and the astonishment which a picture of his had excited in him, he repaired to Rome, where, by an unremitted study of the Farnese gallery, which he copied exactly, he acquired a correct style of design, and became a successful follower of the Carracci. On his return to Naples he availed himself of these acquirements to establish his reputation, as well as to maintain it on certain occasions when he had to contend with others; as, for instance, in a Madonna at S. Anna de' Lombardi; in a S. Carlò at the church of S. Agnello; and in the Christ bearing his Cross at the hospital of Incurables,—pictures, which connoisseurs have extolled as most happy imitations of Annibal Carracci's manner. For the rest, we may recognize the school of Caravaggio in the strong lights and shades of most of his other works. He was an elaborate rather than a hasty painter. There exist, however, some works of his in so poor a style, that Dominici thinks he either purposely painted them so to spite those who would not pay him a high price, or else delivered them over to Mercurio d'Aversa, a pupil of his, and not one of the best.

The three painters whom I have here described in succession, were the three authors of the unceasing persecution, to which those foreign artists, who had either settled at Naples of their own accord, or been invited thither, were for several years exposed. Bellisario had managed to acquire a sovereign jurisdiction, or rather, a tyrannical sway over the Neapolitan painters, partly by means of his reputation, partly by artifice, partly by violence. All the more lucrative orders he took care to secure to himself, recommending for the execution of the rest one or other of the many artists dependent upon him, who were for the most part of an inferior stamp. The Cav. Massimo, Santafede, and other more distinguished artists, if they were not dependent upon him, at least avoided coming to an open rupture with him; dreading him as a man of a treacherous and vindictive temper, capable of committing the blackest crimes; one who, out of envy, had even administered poison to Luigi Rodrigo, the most promising and the most amiable of his pupils.

To maintain his preeminence, it became necessary for Belisario to exclude, not so much those foreigners who painted in oil, as those who painted in fresco. In the year 1609, Annibal Caracci repaired thither for the purpose of decorating the church of Spirito Santo and that of [illegible], for which he finished a small picture as a sort of specimen of his style. The Greek and his adherents being called upon to give an opinion of this exquisite painting, unanimously pronounced it an insipid performance, and declared that its author could have no genius for works on a large scale: hence, that inimitable artist returned to Rome during the hottest period of the year, where he shortly afterwards died. But the work in which foreigners met with the greatest opposition, was that of the royal chapel of St. Januarius, which, even while he was employed on painting the choir of the Certosa, a committee of managers had resolved to entrust to D'Arpino. Belisario, therefore, leaguing with Spagnoletto (a man like himself, of a haughty and overbearing temper) and Caracciolo, both of whom aspired to the task, led D'Arpino so uneasy a life, that, before he had finished the choir on which he was engaged, he fled to Monte Casino, and from thence returned to Rome. The work was then given to Guido: no long time, however, had elapsed before two unknown individuals assaulted that artist's servant, and, for himself, sent to him to say that he must either prepare for death, or quit Naples forthwith; as he accordingly did. Gessi, a scholar of Guido's, was not to be intimidated by this example; but having applied for and obtained the honourable employment, he repaired to Naples with two assistants, Gio. Batista Ruggieri and Lorenzo Menini. These artists were treacherously invited on board a galley under pretence of inspecting it, when, the vessel putting to sea on the instant, they were transported to some distant place, to the great grief of their master, who, notwithstanding the inquiries he caused to be made after them even at Rome, could hear no tidings of them all the while he remained at Naples.

In consequence of this event, Guido himself having also quitted Naples, the committee, losing all hope of succeeding in their endeavours, were now beginning to yield to this cabal of monopolists: assigning the fresco-works to Corenzio and Caracciolo, and giving Spagnoletto good reason to expect that he should be employed on the altar-pieces; when on a sudden, repenting of the determination they had come to, they caused all that had been executed by the two former painters to be effaced, and committed the decoration of the chapel in all its parts to Domenichino. To the honour of these upright and liberal persons, be it observed, that they engaged to pay him one hundred ducats for every full-length figure, fifty for every half-length, and five-and-twenty for every head. They moreover took steps to ensure his quiet; prevailing upon the viceroy to threaten the cabal with his displeasure in case any molestation should be offered to him. But this was doing nothing. It was little that they attempted to make Domenichino pass for a cold and insipid painter, and to discredit him among those who see only with their eyes,—a numerous class in every place. They harassed him by calumnies, by anonymous letters, by defacing his paintings, by mixing ashes with the lime, in order to make the plaster crack and fall down; and, with a refinement in malice, got the viceroy to engage him to paint certain pictures for the court of Madrid. These pictures, while as yet little more than mere daubs, were abstracted from his studio and carried to court; where Spagnoletto ordered him to retouch them here and there, and, without giving him time to finish them, forwarded them to their destination. The overbearing conduct of his rival; the complaints of the committee, who always met with some fresh obstacle to the completion of the work; and the suspicion of some sinister design, at length determined Domenichino to set off secretly for Rome, in the hope that he might from thence order matters better. The reports of his flight being at length hushed up, and fresh measures taken for his safety, he returned and resumed his labours in the chapel, where he executed the paintings on the walls and drum of the cupola, and even made considerable progress in the altar-pieces.

Before he could finish his task, however, he was overtaken by death, hastened either by poison, or by the cruel vexations he had experienced both from his relations and his rivals; the concern of which was filled up by the arrival of his old enemy Lanfranco. The latter supplied the place of Zampieri in the works on the cupola of the chapel; Spagnoletto succeeded him in one of the oil paintings, and the Cav. Stanzioni in the other; while each of them, stimulated by the love of fame, if he did not surpass, at least rivalled Domenichino. Caracciolo was now no more. Bellisario, on account of his advanced age, took no part in the work: nor was it long, ere, having mounted a scaffolding for the purpose of retouching some of his frescos, he fell headlong from it and was killed. Nor did Spagnoletto experience a very enviable fate; for, becoming insupportable even to himself, and anxious to shun the public eye, on account of having had a daughter seduced, as well as through remorse at the unworthy persecutions which he had abetted, he embarked on board a vessel; nor, if we credit the Neapolitan accounts, is it known whither he fled, or to what end he came. Palomino makes him to have died at Naples itself in the year 1656, at the age of sixty-seven, but still does not state him to have escaped the afflictions above recorded. Thus did these three ambitious men, who either by violence or treachery had baffled the generosity and taste of so many noble patrons, and rendered so many eminent artists the sport of a mournful and eventful tragedy, in the last act of it reap but bitter fruits from all their unworthy machinations. And impartial posterity, that sees Domenichino preferred before them all, should draw from it this inference, that whoever founds his own reputation or his own fortune on the depression of another's merit, builds upon the sand.*

IL CALABRESE.

GUERCINO himself was never at Naples; but the Cav. Mattia Preti, commonly called the Cav. Calabrese, allured by the novelty of his style, repaired to Cento, and put himself under his tuition. This we learn from Dominici, who had heard him say, that, as far as regarded actual instruction, his master was Guercino; but that, as far as regarded his own private studies, it might be said that every eminent artist was his master: and in fact he had visited many different countries; observing and studying the most celebrated works of every school both in and out of Italy. Hence it was with him in painting as it often is in point of conversation with those who have travelled much, who, start what subject you will, are usually found to throw some new light upon it: and ac-

* One of the most eminent of the Neapolitan imitators of the Calabrese, was the Cav. Massimo Stanzioni.

ceedingly. Even when displays great variety and originality in the dresses, the ornaments, and the images that he represents. He was twenty-six years of age before he attempted colouring, contenting himself till then with acquiring experience in design. In this branch of art he possessed considerable merit; not so much, however, in the representation of delicate figures, as in those of a bolder and more robust character; though even in these he sometimes degenerates into heaviness. In like manner, his colouring is more remarkable for strength than for beauty; presenting us with a chiaroscuro that makes his figures start from the canvas with all the effect of relief, and a sort of general ashy tinge admirably suited to subjects of a tragical and melancholy cast. Hence that here by his forte he delighted to represent martyrdoms, murders, plagues, or the compassionate visitings of [illegible]; such were the subjects he most frequently handled.

He executed some large frescos at Modena, Naples, and Malta. In the church of S. Andrea della Valle at Rome, where, under the tribune of Domenichino, he painted three large historical pieces of the Titular Saint, he was less successful. The work suffers by comparison with Domenichino's; not to mention that the figures are disproportioned to the place, and are on the side of heaviness. In Italy his oil paintings are almost innumerable; a circumstance to be attributed to his very long life, his great rapidity of execution, and the habit he was in of leaving some memento of himself wherever he went, now and then in the churches, but more commonly in private collections; and these are for the most part historical subjects, containing half-length figures after the manner of Guercino or Caravaggio. Not only Naples, but Rome and Florence also, abound with his pictures, and Bologna more perhaps than either of them. In the Ercolani palace is his Belisarius in the character of a beggar; in that of the Ratti a Holy Penitent with a chain that forces him to assume a most uneasy posture; in one of the Malvezzi palaces a Sir Thomas More in prison; in that of the Ercolani a [illegible]; besides others, as well as those in certain other collections of the nobility. One of the most studied of his altarpieces is at the cathedral of Siena; it is a S. Bernardino in the act of preaching to, and converting, the people. At Naples he painted a great deal besides the ceiling of the Celestini church, though less than he himself and all other artists of correct taste could have wished; who, indeed, made common cause with him in resisting the innovations of Giordano. Giordano's star, however, still maintained the ascendant over that of every other artist; insomuch that, in spite of his faults, he triumphed over them all. Even Preti himself was constrained to quit the field, and end his days at Malta; where, out of regard to his great merit as a painter, he was made a commendatore of the Maltese Order.*

NEAPOLITAN SCHOOL.

EPOCH IV.

GIORDANO, SOLIMENA, &c.

It was somewhat after the middle of the seventeenth century that Luca Giordano began to make a figure at Naples. This artist, though his style was not the best of the age in which he lived, yet surpassed all his contemporaries in good fortune,—the consequence of a genius at once vast, bold, and creative, which Marotta regarded as altogether unique and unexampled. These splendid endowments began to develop themselves even in his childhood. His father Antonio placed him at first under the tuition of Ribera, then sent

* [illegible]

him to Rome to profit by the instructions of Cortona, and having afterwards familiarized him with all the best schools of Italy, brought him back again to Naples, enriched with designs, and his mind well stored with ideas. His father was but an indifferent painter, who, though he had nothing to depend upon at Rome but the exertions of his son, whose designs were even then in very great request, had no other precept to give him than that which necessity dictated; that is to use despatch (*di far presto*). A certain writer records the following unexampled circumstance:—that Luca, when about to take refreshment, was not used to desist from his work, but that opening his mouth just as a young blackbird or a young sparrow would have done, his father filled it with food, singing all the while the *Luca fa presto* in his ears. Accordingly, *Luca fa presto* was the nick-name by which he went among his fellow-students at Rome; and such too is the name not unfrequently given to him in the history of art. By constantly inculcating this principle, Antonio accustomed his son to a most portentous celerity of execution; whence he has been sometimes called the *Fulmine della pittura*. True indeed it is, that this amazing rapidity of execution was not owing so much to dexterity of hand, as to quickness of conception, as Solimene often used to observe,—a faculty that enabled him to group the whole subject at once, and made it quite unnecessary for him to stop during the progress of his work to look for expedients, exempting him from the doubts and hesitation and corrections incident to other artists. He was also called the Proteus of painting, from the extraordinary talent he possessed of counterfeiting the works of others; the effect even this of a retentive memory, which nothing that he had once seen ever escaped. Of this imitative faculty we have still many proofs in pictures painted by him in the style of Albert Durer, Bassan, Titian, and Rubens, which he used to pass off for originals, not only with connoisseurs, but even with his rivals, who had been warned that they ought also to be on their guard against him. Pictures of this kind have since fetched more than double or triple the price of one in Giordano's usual style. Of these there are specimens even in the churches of Naples, as, for instance, the two pictures in the style of Guido, at S. Teresa, more especially that of the Nativity of Christ.

None of these styles, however, did he adopt as his own. At first he betrayed marks of affecting Spagnoletto's manner; subsequently, as in a picture of the Passion at the above-mentioned S. Teresa, he followed pretty closely that of Paul Veronese; indeed, he ever retained that master's maxim of exciting admiration and attracting the eye by a studied introduction of ornament. From Cortona he seems to have adopted the love of contrast and the broad masses of light that characterize his compositions, as well as the frequent repetition of the same features, which in his female figures he often copied from those of his wife. For the rest, he sought to distinguish himself from every other master by a novel method of colouring. In this he was not very solicitous to conform to the more received principles of art: his colouring is in general too little in accordance with truth and reality, but more especially in his chiaroscuro, where he pursued a system much too arbitrary and ideal. It delights us nevertheless by a certain gracefulness and illusiveness of character, which few attend to and none find it easy to imitate. Nor did he in this respect hold himself up as a model to his scholars: on the contrary, he reproved them whenever they attempted to imitate him; telling them that it was not the part of tyros to penetrate into views of that sort He was well enough acquainted with the laws of design, but too careless in his observance of them; and it is Dominici's opinion, that if he had ob served them rigidly, that fire, which now constitutes his chief merit, would have cooled,—an excuse which will hardly appear satisfactory to every reader. The following, perhaps, will be considered as the truer reason;—that being greedy of gain, and therefore ready to undertake works even for the lower orders, he was led to abuse his facility of execution even to the prejudice of his reputation. Hence, too, he is charged with having often painted in a superficial manner, laying on his colours too lightly, and diluting them too much with oil; a circumstance which has caused his pictures prematurely to exhibit symptoms of decay.

Giordano's works abound in Naples both in public and private: there is scarcely a church in that great city which cannot boast of possessing a specimen of his works. The Driving out from the Temple those who bought and sold therein, in the possession of the Padri Girolamini,—a piece, the architectural ornaments of which are said to be the work of Moscatiello, a celebrated perspective painter,—is much admired. Of all his fresco paintings, those in the treasury of the Certosa are the most esteemed. These were executed by him at a rather advanced age, and seem to combine all the best properties of his style. The Lifting up of the Serpent in the Desert, and the crowds of Israelites who turn to it as the appointed means of escape from the pangs inflicted by the Serpents' bite, is an astonishing work; so are also the other works on the walls and on the ceiling, all of which are taken from Scripture. The cupola of S. Brigida is also much extolled; it was executed in competition with Francesco di Maria, with such rapidity and in such fascinating colours, that with the many it caused him to be preferred before that erudite master, and thus paved the way for a less correct taste among the rising generation. The picture of S. Saverio, too, painted for the church of that name in the short space of a day and a half—a picture abounding in figures, and in point of colouring equal to any thing he ever produced—is also looked upon as a miracle of art. Giordano visited Florence for the purpose of painting the Corsini chapel and the Riccardi gallery; to say nothing of the works he executed for various churches as well as for private individuals, more especially for the noble family of Rome, where were those Bacchanals of his which were afterwards transferred to the Capponi palace. He also wrought for the Grand Duke; and Cosmo III., in whose presence he both designed and coloured a large picture almost in less time than another would have taken to talk about it, complimented him as the very painter for a sovereign prince. The same compliment was paid him by Charles II. of Spain, at whose court he was employed for thirteen years; though, to judge from the number of pictures he left behind him, one would say that he had there spent a long life. At length, when he had now attained a good old age, he returned to his native country, and died there shortly afterwards lamented as the greatest painter of his time.

His school produced but few that were eminent in design; the greater part of his scholars abusing their master's maxim,—that he is a good painter who contrives to please the public, and that the public is more taken with colouring than with design.*

SOLIMENE.

Francesco Solimene, surnamed L'Abate Ciccio, born at Nocera de' Pagani, was the son of Angelo, a scholar of the Cav. Massimo. Feeling a strong propensity for painting, he soon quitted his other studies, received the rudiments of the art from his father, and repaired to Naples. There he placed

* The most distinguished of Giordano's scholars was Paolo de' Matteis. It was his [illegible] boast that he had completed the painting of a large cupola, like that of the Gesù Nuovo, in sixty-six days; which cupola was a few years since taken down, [illegible]

himself under the tuition of Francesco di Maria, who, according to him, devoted himself too exclusively to design; quitting him, therefore, he took to frequenting the academy of Po; where, with all the ardour of youth, he applied himself at once to design the naked figure and to colour it. Thus he may rather be called the scholar of all the eminent artists whose works he copied and studied continually, than of any one in particular. At first he closely imitated Cortona; and even after he had adopted a manner of his own, he still looked up to that master as a model; so much so, indeed, as to borrow whole figures from his works; taking care, however, to accommodate them to his own style. This new and characteristic style of Solimena's approaches nearer to Preti's than to that of any one else; the design, indeed, is not so correct, nor is the colouring so true, but the heads possess greater beauty; in these he sometimes imitates Guido, sometimes Maratta, and not unfrequently copies them from nature. Hence, by some he has been called the Cav. Calabrese "ammanierato" (ingentilito.) To Preti he added another model, Lanfranco, whom he used to call his master, and from whom he derived that intricacy (aggruppamento) of composition which he may perhaps be said to have carried to excess. From these two also he derived that strong chiaroscuro perceptible in the works which he executed in the prime of life; for as he advanced in years he neglected it, and adopted an easier and sweeter style. In each of his works he finished the whole of the design, and carefully compared it with nature before he began to colour it: so that, as far as regards the preparatory steps, he may be reckoned among the most accurate painters, at his better days at least; for he was afterwards too studious of facility, and opened the way to mannerism. In literature he displayed the same facility and elegance that procured him a distinguished place among the poets of his day. To his praise also it may be said, that he aimed at universality in the art, employing his pencil in every branch comprised within the whole compass of painting—portraits, historical pieces, landscapes, animals, fruits, together with the ornaments of architecture and manufactures. To whatever department he applied himself, he seemed to have been purposely formed for it. As he lived to the age of ninety, and was endowed with great rapidity of execution, his works have been scattered over all Europe, almost in as great abundance as those of Giordano. Of that artist he was at once the competitor and the friend; inferior to him in genius, but chaster in style. When Giordano was no more, Solimena, who, (notwithstanding all that his rivals might please to say as to the want of truth in his colouring,) well knew that there who now no longer any one to dispute the palm with him in Italy, began to set an extravagant price upon his pictures, and nevertheless was kept in constant employment.

Among the works that do him most credit, is that in the sacristy of the Padri Teatini of San Paolo Maggiore; a work consisting of various historical pieces. His pictures also on the arches of the different chapels at the church of the Holy Apostles, are also worthy of being recorded. Of his exquisite finishing we may take as an example the chapel of St. Philip at the church dell' Oratorio, where every figure looks as if it had been the work of a miniature painter. Except in the Neapolitan State, his works are not often to be met with in private collections. The Albani and Colonna galleries at Rome contain a few historical pieces of his; that of the Buonaccorsi family at Macerata, a somewhat greater number from profane story; and among them the Death of Dido, a picture on a large scale and of admirable effect. The largest work of his that I have met with in the Ecclesiastical State, is a Last Supper in the refectory of the Conventuals of Assisi; an elegant and exquisitely finished piece, where, among the attendants, the artist has given us a portrait of himself.

VENETIAN SCHOOL.

EPOCH I.

It is only subsequent to the year 1300 that we meet with the names and the works of Venetian painters united;* about which time, partly owing to the example of Giotto, partly owing to their own industry and talents, these painters, both in Venice itself and its dependencies, adopted a better and more graceful style. The merit of the Venetian painters, however, became more strikingly manifest during the fifteenth century,† that period which gradually paved the way for the noble style of Giorgione and Titian. After the

* Of the painters who lived previous to the above-mentioned period, [illegible]

† [illegible]

middle of that century, the generality of painters evinced here a taste not unlike what I have already described as existing in other countries,—divested rather of the rudeness which characterises the old masters, than embellished by the elegance of the moderns. Although, even at that early period, canvas was in as general use at Venice, as panel was elsewhere, still, painting in water colours was the only method yet known,—an admirable method as regards the durability of the tints, (inasmuch that some specimens have come down to our days unimpaired,) but incompatible with a perfect blending and softness of colouring. At length the secret of painting in oil was brought to us from Flanders, by Antonello of Messina; an event which led to a happier era among the schools of Italy, especially that of Venice, which profited by it more, and, in all probability, earlier than any of the rest.

In the Venetian, as in every other school, the artists who flourished during this period retain some vestiges of the hard dry manner of the old masters; frequently copying nature with all her imperfections; as, for instance, in figures of an excessively tall and slender make. For the rest, where their proportions are truer, they arrest the attention by that correctness, simplicity, and carefulness of design, which seems, as it were, to evince a dread of exaggeration. One might almost

they seem to have been educated in the school of those more ancient Greek sculptors, whose works delight us as much by their truth, as do those of others by their sublimity. This air of truth and reality more especially distinguishes their heads, which, for the most part, are portraits copied from the life, taken either from among the populace, or from among men eminent for learning, or dignity, or military exploits; and to this practice, which was familiar even to the artists of the thirteenth century, we owe not a few of those heads which Giovio caused to be copied for his museum, and which have since found their way into almost every country either in pictures or prints. Frequently, too, at that early period, the painter introduced his own portrait into the picture; a species of adulation which went into disuse as cultivation advanced in Italy.

Their very colours are remarkable for truth and simplicity; though not always properly blended, particularly with the grounds, nor sufficiently broken into lights and shades; and yet more remarkable for simplicity is the composition of their altar-pieces. In these they rarely introduced historical subjects, contenting themselves at that early period with representing the Virgin on a throne, surrounded by such a retinue of Saints as the devotion of the times deemed indispensable. Nor did they represent these, as hereafter, still and stiff, equidistant from each other, and in unmeaning attitudes; they made some attempt at contrast; for while one was looking toward the Virgin, another would be seen reading a book; or if the former happened to be on his knees, the latter would be seen standing upright. The national temper, always sprightly and jocund, developed itself even then in a brilliancy of colouring surpassing that of every other school; while, perhaps for the very purpose of giving greater relief to these brilliantly coloured figures, they painted their skies of a pale, languid hue. They did their utmost, too, to enliven their compositions with pleasing figures, seizing every opportunity to introduce sportive cherubs into their sacred pieces, and vying with each other in the life and movement with which they invested them, some of them in the act of singing, others playing upon different instruments, and not unfrequently placing in their hands well-woven baskets containing fruits and flowers, moistened, one would almost think, with recent dew. In the drapery of their figures they adhered to nature; avoiding that trite and closely-folded drapery, and that bandaging of the body, which characterises Mantegna's works, and found its way into other schools.

Nor did they lay small stress upon certain accessories of art, such as their thrones, which they formed in the richest and most splendid style; their landscapes, which they drew with an astonishing degree of truth; and their architectural ornaments, which they frequently introduced after the fashion of a portico or a tribune. Sometimes, too, we find that, accommodating themselves to the stone-work and structure of the altar, they gave a fictitious continuation of it within the picture; and with so close a resemblance of colour and style did they do it, as to deceive the eye, and make us doubt where the external ornament ends and where the picture begins.

GIAN BELLINI.

This improvement of style was the work of Gian Bellini more than any other master. In the vast number of works which he produced, extending from before the year 1464 down to the year 1516, he presents us with a sort of graduated scale of his own progress, which was in fact the progress of his school. His very first pictures, which are in water colours, evince his ambition to introduce into his country an improved and more elevated style. The larger palace of the Cornaro family, where, in the time of the Queen of Cyprus, his pencil was frequently employed, contain various pictures in his first manner, as well as others of a later date, the latest being always the most beautiful: among them is a St. Francis in the midst of a dense thicket; a piece that might excite the envy of the most accomplished landscape painter. In the year 1488, the year in which he painted the altar-piece that is still preserved in the sacristy of the Conventuali, we find him exciting the commendation even of Vasari both for tastefulness of manner and correctness of design. In a still happier manner did he execute some other works, after he had witnessed certain specimens of Giorgione's. From that period he displayed greater novelty of invention, imparted greater roundness to his figures, and greater warmth to his colouring; his transition too, from one colour to another, became more natural and easy, his representation of those parts of the figure exposed to view more correct, his drapery more majestic: had he acquired a perfect softness and delicacy of contour, (which, however, he never attained to,) he might have been proposed as an accomplished model of the modern style. Certainly neither Pietro Perugino, Ghirlandaio, nor Mantegna, approached so near to it. The amateur may meet with many specimens of his works both at Venice and elsewhere. He should not neglect to observe the altar-piece at St. Zacharias of the date of 1505, and that at St.

Giobbe of 1510; nor should he neglect to see the Bacchanal of the Villa Aldobrandini at Rome, painted in 1514, which, in consequence of his advanced age, he left in an unfinished state. Other pictures of his have I met with of great merit, though without date,—a picture of the Virgin at the cathedral of Bergamo, a Baptism of our Saviour at S. Corona of Vicenza, an Infant Jesus asleep on the Virgin's knees between two Angels,—the latter a most bewitching picture preserved in a cabinet at the Capuchins of Venice. It exhibits a rare union of beauty, grace, and expression; qualities of which, as regards this school, he may be called the father. He seems to have continued his labours even to his latest years; there being in the choice collection of St. Justina, at Padua, a Madonna of the date of 1516. Figures of the Virgin and of the Dead Christ are the pictures of his that we most frequently meet with.

GENTILE BELLINI.

The name of Giovanni must not be dissevered from that of his brother Gentile, who preceded him alike in the period of his birth and of his death.

These two Bellini lived apart, but always on the most brotherly terms; treating one another as friends, mutually commending each other, and each esteeming the other as superior to himself,—a circumstance which proves Giovanni's modesty, while it displays Gentile's justice. To the latter, nature had been less prodigal of her gifts; but diligence, which sometimes supplies the place of genius, procured him an honourable station among his contemporaries. Though very inferior to his brother, and in many of his works betraying vestiges of the hard dry manner of the old masters, yet he has produced some that are very beautiful;—as the histories of the Holy Cross, at S. Giovanni, and the Preaching of St. Mark at the school of that name; a piece which, though placed near a work of Paris Bordone's, scarcely suffers by comparison. In Gentile we recognize a faithful copyist, capable of transferring to his canvass whatever attracted his attention in a crowded assembly. The features of the audience, as well as the make of their bodies, display all the variety that we meet with in nature, without even excepting those instances of deformity, into which, from the generality of her laws, nature must sometimes fall; such as the bald head, the big belly, and other imperfections; and what is yet more worthy of observation, St. Mark's hearers are, without any regard to the manifest anachronism, clothed in the garb of Venetians or Turks. Still, however, as all is correctly drawn from nature, judiciously arranged, and invested with much spirit and animation, this work is not without considerable attractions. I may even go further, and affirm, that some pictures of this artist, on a small scale, which he seems to have executed *con amore*, would do no discredit even to his brother. Such is the Presentation of the Infant Jesus in the Temple, in the Barbarigo palace at S. Polo,—a picture consisting of half-length figures, repeated with still greater care and delicacy in the Grimani palace. Here Gentile's picture has a beautiful work of Gian Bellini's opposite to it; and though the former is confessedly inferior to the latter in softness and mellowness of colouring, yet in beauty and the other graces of art it is preferred before it.*

* The other more distinguished artists of this epoch omitted in this abridgment are,—Vittore Carpaccio—Pellegrino di S. Daniello—Jacopo Montagnana—Francesco da Ponte, the father of Bassano—the two Montagna—Giovanni Bonconsigli, styled Il Marescalco—and Andrea Previtali.

VENETIAN SCHOOL.

EPOCH II.

GIORGIONE, TITIAN, TINTORETTO, BASSANO, PAUL VERONESE, &c.

We are now arrived at the brightest era of the Venetian school, in which, as in every other, the best artists flourished about the beginning of the sixteenth century; men, who not only eclipsed the fame of their predecessors, but even deprived their successors of all chance of equalling them. To attain to this unrivalled eminence, they pursued, as we shall see in the sequel, different paths; all of them, however, conspiring in their efforts to surpass every other school in truth and brilliance of colouring,—an attribute which they bequeathed to their followers, and one which forms the distinguishing characteristic of the Venetian painters. In the art of colouring, the more celebrated Venetians conformed in some degree to the system pursued by the other great Italian painters, while in some degree they departed from it. It was at that time a common practice to give the panel or canvass proposed to be painted a covering consisting of a preparation of chalk; and this white ground, which was favourable to every colour the painter could lay on, contributed to invest them with that lucid richness, that bloom, and astonishing transparency, for which they are so remarkable. The above custom which, owing to avarice and sloth, had gone into disuse, is now fortunately coming into vogue once more. But besides this, the Venetians had a method which may be called peculiarly their own. For, during these three centuries, that which has principally served to distinguish the greater part of the Venetian painters is, not that they laid on their colours thicker than others, but that they laid them on by separate strokes of the pencil, ([illegible]) and that each colour being thus placed in its proper situation, without doing it violence or taking much pains to rub it in, they went on continually heightening its effect, in order that each tint might remain pure and unmixed,—a work which requires not only quickness of hand and head, but early initiation and constant practice. Hence Vecchia was wont to say, that any pains-taking painter might contrive to copy the best finished pictures of others; but that to copy the works of Titian and Paul Veronese, and imitate their pencillings, was a task in which none could succeed except such as were Venetians either by birth or at least by education.—(Boschini, p. [illegible].) Should it be asked, what are the advantages of this method, I answer, that Boschini points out two important ones. The first is, that by this mode of colouring, harshness of style is more easily avoided; the second, that this method more than any other tends to make the picture distinct at a distance; and as pictures are not designed to be placed close to the eye, but to be viewed at some distance, the object is thus more easily attained. Nor were any artists better acquainted with the affinity between different colours; insomuch that their very method of placing them in juxtaposition and contrasting them, may be considered as another source of the charming and brilliant effect produced by their works, more especially those of Titian and his contemporaries.

This skilfulness of representation was not confined merely to their fleshes, in the colour of which the followers of Titian have more particularly surpassed every other school. It extended also to the drapery; there being no variety of velvet, stuff, or crape, which they have not imitated to admiration, especially in their highly-decorated portraits, which were then all the rage among the Venetians. Indeed, to this sort of exercise, which compels the artist to be both faithful to nature and studious of effect, we may in some measure attribute the remarkable truth and force to which these consummate colourists attained. They were, moreover, eminently successful in imitating all sorts of work in gold, silver, or other metals; insomuch that in no part do we meet of such splendid palaces or such costly banquets as we meet with in the pictures of the Venetian school. They distinguished themselves, too, in landscapes, in which they have sometimes surpassed the Florentine painters; and not less in their architectural ornaments, which they introduced into their compositions with a peculiar dignity unknown elsewhere,—a practice admirably adapted to facilitate the disposition of the groups of their figures as well as to give them variety and effect.

These and other qualities of the like kind which enchant the eye, and equally delight the learned and the unlearned, and which by their novelty and fidelity of representation transport us in idea to the scene before us, constitute a style to which Reynolds has given the name of Ornamental. That English critic assigns it the next place after the sublime style, and remarks that those who cultivated the latter seem to have shunned all showy and ambitious ornament, both because it diverts the painter's attention from design and expression, and because even in the spectator it produces but a transient pleasure which seldom reaches the heart. The sublime of Michael Angelo and Raphael, without much courting the attention by studied decoration, goes at once to the heart; like

you with terror, or inspires you with courage; awakens in you emotions of piety, of veneration, and a love of right; exalts you in some measure above yourself, and even against your will excites in you the most delightful of all feelings—that of wonder.

Let it not, however, be imagined, that the sole merit of the Venetians consists in the exquisite beauty of their colouring and decoration; or that the more noble style and true method of painting was unknown in these parts. Indeed, this school has been most prolific not only of painters, but of admirable specimens in every department of the art; but neither are these painters nor these specimens so well known as they deserve to be.

GIORGIONE.

The golden age of Venetian painting commences with Giorgione and Titian. Between these two, who were both companions and rivals, the greater number of artists, both in the capital and its dependent territory, were in some sort divided; one city taking one for its model, another the other. Giorgione Barbarelli di Castelfranco was more commonly called Giorgione, from a certain elevation of mind and largeness of stature with which nature had endowed him; a character also which he stamped upon his works, as sometimes happens in the case of authors, whose writings furnish us with an image of themselves. Even while he was yet a pupil of Bellini's, impressed with a consciousness of his own powers, he avoided that littleness of manner which was not yet wholly abandoned, substituting in its stead a freedom and a sort of licence, which constitutes the perfection of art. In this respect he has the merit of originality; till his time no one had attained that masterly boldness and strength of pencilling, so well calculated to strike the spectator at a distance. He afterwards went on continually improving in elevation of style, displaying greater fulness of manner, greater novelty of foreshortening, greater vivacity both of countenance and attitude, greater choice of drapery as well as of other accessories, greater truth and delicacy of transition from one colour to another; and lastly, far greater force and effect in his chiaroscuro. In this latter quality it was that Venetian painting was then most deficient;—for, before the beginning of the sixteenth century, it had been introduced into other schools by Da Vinci. And accordingly, from this same Da Vinci, or, to speak more correctly, from certain designs and works of Da Vinci, Vasari will have it that Giorgione derived it; a fact which Zanetti will by no means admit, contending that on this point also Giorgione was in the strictest sense original. And to say the truth, the style of Leonardo and of the Milanese artists, his scholars, not only differs from that of Giorgione in design, affecting the slender and the graceful, while the latter delights in the full and the rotund; but differs from it also in chiaroscuro. Leonardo evinces a greater predilection for shadow, which he goes on gradually diminishing with great care; while, with regard to his light, he diffuses it more sparingly, seeking to make it fall on a confined space with a brightness calculated to produce a powerful effect. Giorgione's manner is more open and less overcharged with shadow, nor do his middle tints ever betray anything of a greyish or iron tinge, being remarkable for truth and beauty: in short, if Mengs is correct in his opinion, his style bears a stronger resemblance to Correggio's than to that of any other master. Still I cannot admit that Da Vinci did not in any degree contribute to Giorgione's new style. Every improvement in painting has originated with some one individual, who, attracting admiration by novelty of manner, has, by his example, taught such as were within his own sphere, and by his reputation, such as were more distant, what it was that was still wanting to art; and hence have certain geniuses here and there started up calculated to improve it still further in this respect. Thus, if I mistake not, it happened in the case of perspective after the time of Pier della Francesca; in that of foreshortening, after Melozzo; and in like manner, in that of chiaroscuro, after Leonardo.

Giorgione's works consisted in great measure of frescos painted on the façades of houses, especially at Venice, of which there now exist only some few relics, as if to make us regret the loss of the rest. On the contrary, both there and elsewhere we meet with many oil paintings of his in private hands in the very highest preservation; a circumstance to be attributed to his laying on the colours with a full, well-fed pencil. His portraits are more especially admirable for the mind he has contrived to throw into them, for the style of the heads, the contrivance of the dresses, the arrangement of the hair, the plumes, the armour, and the exquisite imitation of the flesh itself; to which, though he usually employed colours of a glowing and highly sanguine hue, he imparted such a degree of grace, that after a thousand imitators he still stands alone. On analyzing these colours, Ridolfi found that, like the manner of the ancient Greeks, they were few in number, and unalloyed by those orange, grey, and azure tints, which were afterwards introduced to the prejudice of natural effect. Historical pieces by him are very rare; as the Dead Christ in the Monte di Pietà at Trevigi; the S

Omobono in the Scuola de' Sarti at Venice; or the Calming of the Tempest by the same Saint in that of St. Mark, where, amongst other things, are three naked gondoliers, highly esteemed both for design and attitude. Milan possesses two of an oblong shape, containing several figures on a scale somewhat larger than Poussin's, which may be said to have more of fulness than beauty. The first is at the Ambrosian library, the second at the archbishop's palace, and, with some, passes for the finest *Giorgione* in the world. It represents the Taking of the Infant Moses out of the Nile, and his Presentation to the daughter of Pharaoh. The colours are few in number, but being well distributed, well blended, and well broken into light and shade, they present the eye with a severe kind of harmony, resembling, if I may so say, that arising from a simple but well-set air, which often affords us greater pleasure than pieces of a more noisy and complicated kind.

Giorgione died in the year 1511, at the age of thirty-four. Thus the Venetians were obliged to seek instruction rather from his works than from any scholars he could have formed.

FRA SEBASTIANO.

THE most celebrated of Giorgione's scholars is Sebastiano, a Venetian, who, from the habit he assumed, and the office to which he was afterwards appointed at Rome, was called Fra Sebastiano del Piombo. Leaving Gian Bellini, he became a disciple of Giorgione's, and succeeded better than any other artist in imitating the tone and lucid richness of his colouring. An altar-piece of his at S. Gio. Grisostomo passed with some for a work of his master's, so closely does it resemble his style. It may, perhaps, fairly be presumed that he was assisted in the composition of it; for it is notorious that Sebastiano was not blessed with much fertility of invention; and that in pieces comprising many figures, he was slow and irresolute; prodigal of promises, but loath to begin, and still more loath to finish his pictures. Hence historical subjects or altar-pieces of his are rarely to be met with; such as the Nativity of the Virgin at S. Agostino of Perugia, or the Flagellation at the Osservanti of Viterbo, deemed the best picture in that city. Cabinet pictures, and more especially portraits, he executed in considerable number and without much difficulty; nor is it easy to meet with hands more beautifully executed, flesh of a more rosy hue, or other accessories of a more attractive nature. Thus, in his portrait of Pietro Aretino, we may distinguish in the dress no less than five different shades of black—accurate imitations of velvet, satin, and other materials. Being invited to Rome by Agostino Chigi, and looked up to as one of the first colourists of his day, he was employed to paint in competition with Peruzzi and Raphael himself; and in one of the saloons of the Farnesina, then called the Chigi palace, we may still see the rival works of these three masters.

Sebastiano soon perceived that, with such men for his competitors, his own style of design could not appear to much advantage, and therefore set about improving it; but he sometimes fell into hardness, owing to the restraint it imposed upon him. In this respect he was in some of his works assisted by Michael Angelo, after whose designs he painted the Pietà at the Conventuali of Viterbo, and the Transfiguration and the other pictures at S. Pietro in Montorio, which cost him the labour of six years. Vasari tells us, that Michael Angelo united with him for the purpose of counteracting the partiality evinced at Rome for Raphael. He adds that, when the latter was no more, the palm was, owing to Michael Angelo's influence, universally awarded to Sebastiano; and that Giulio Ro-

gione, and the rest of the great school, were all boys in the back ground. I know not that I am called upon to give an opinion on an assertion which, if we disbelieve it, casts an imputation on the historian, and which, if we admit it, does no great credit to [illegible]. I leave it therefore to the reader to draw his own conclusions. Sebastiano was the inventor of a new method of painting in oils on stone, and in this manner painted the Flagellation at St. Peter's in Montorio,—a work as much blackened by time, as the frescoes which he executed in the same church are well preserved. He also executed cabinet pictures on stone, a practice highly esteemed at that early period, but soon abandoned in consequence of the difficulty of removing them. In this, or some such manner, were executed a few pictures of the sixteenth century, which in certain museums now-a-days pass for genuine antiques.

Those who follow are referred by history to the school of Giorgione, not as pupils, but as imitators. They all retain something of Bellini's style; for, till the time of Tintoretto, the Venetians did not so much aim at making new discoveries, as at perfecting what had already been made; and were less desirous of forgetting the method of the two Bellini, than of modernizing it after the example of Giorgione and Titian. Among the best imitators of Giorgione, we may reckon three artists who were born either at Bergamo or in its vicinity—Lotto, (for he is most commonly held to be a Bergamasque,*) Palma, and Cariani.

LOTTO.

Vasari and others, who mention Lorenzo Lotto, refer him to the Venetian territory generally, without particularizing the place of his birth; and he himself subscribed his S. Cristoforo at Loreto with the words—*Laurentius Lottus pictor Venetus.* A late annotator on Vasari, observing upon the gracefulness of the countenances and the turn of the eyes in his figures, was inclined to believe him a pupil of Da Vinci's; in corroboration of which opinion we may bring forward the authority of Lomazzo, who mentions Cesare de Cesto and Lorenzo Lotto as imitators of Da Vinci in the judicious distribution of light. I cannot, indeed, but think that Lotto would take advantage of his proximity to Milan to become acquainted with, and to imitate, Da Vinci, in certain points; but I

* Federici, in a work published in 1803, shows that Lotto, though usually held to be a Bergamasque, was in reality a Venetian.

do not therefore withhold my assent from history, when it represents him as the scholar of Bellini and the rival of Giorgione. In Lotto's works we discover few if any vestiges of that remarkable uniformity of style perceptible in those of Luini and others of Leonardo's Milanese pupils. His style is, on the whole, strictly Venetian; displaying its strength of colouring, its parade of drapery, and, in his fleshes, the warmth of Giorgione's manner. His pencilling, however, has less of freedom than Giorgione's, whose softness of style he is fond of attempering by the style of the middle time; selecting, at the same time, figures of a lighter make, and imparting to his heads a character of a more placid, and a beauty of a more ideal cast. In the grounds of his pictures he frequently introduces a sort of bright or azure colour, which, if it does not readily blend with the figures, serves at least to give them relief, and to bring them nearer to the eye. He was among the foremost and the most ingenious in inventing new designs for altar-pieces. The St. Antony, in the possession of the Dominicans at Venice, and the St. Nicholas at the Carmine,—an idea which he repeated in the St. Vincent, in the hands of the Dominicans at Recanati, are very novel and original compositions. In his others he does not deviate much from the more usual style of a Madonna seated on a throne and surrounded by saints.

with little angels poised in the air or placed upon the steps; yet even in these he introduces some degree of novelty, either in point of perspective, attitude, or contrast. Thus, in that at S. Bartolommeo of Bergamo, which Ridolfi eulogizes as a most wonderful performance, he represents the Virgin and the Infant Jesus in different postures and on opposite sides of the picture, as though they were addressing the attendant Saints—the former, those on the right hand, the latter, those on the left. So also in that other charming performance at S. Spirito, he introduced an infantine St. John the Baptist, standing at the foot of the throne and holding a lamb in his embrace; in the midst of his caresses evincing a joy so lively, natural, and innocent, with so fascinating a smile playing upon his features, that Raphael or Coreggio could perhaps hardly have produced any thing more beautiful.

These master-pieces of his, and others to be met with in the different churches and collections of Bergamo, place him almost on a level with the first luminaries of art; and if he makes no great figure in Vasari's book, it is because that author had seen only his less studied and less splendid performances. To say the truth, he does not always exhibit the same energy of manner or the same correctness of design. The most brilliant period of his career must, it seems, be computed from the year 1513, when, in preference to many artists of note, he was selected to paint the altar-piece at the Dominicans of Bergamo; and his decline may be dated from the year 1546, the date inscribed on the picture of S. Jacopo dall' Orio at Venice. He also painted some pictures at Ancona, and a considerable number at Recanati in the church of S. Domenico, where, interspersed amidst some masterly performances, (the smaller pictures more especially,) we detect something of carelessness in the extremities, and something of dryness in the composition, after the manner of Giovanni Bellini; whether it be that these were among his earlier works as I must conjecture, or whether they were rather among his latest. For it is notorious, that when he was now advanced in years, he was fond of retiring to Loreto, which is but a short distance from Recanati; where, continually engaged in supplicating the Virgin to lead him into a better path, he ended his days in tranquillity.

PALMA VECCHIO.

JACOPO PALMA, usually styled Palma Vecchio, to distinguish him from his relative Jacopo, becoming enamoured of Giorgione's style, imitated him in the fullness and lucid richness of his colouring; and seems more especially to have had him in his eye, while painting his celebrated S. Barbara at S. Maria Formosa—of all his works the one which exhibits most strength and elevation of character. We meet with some other pictures of his in which he approximates nearer to Titian's manner, from whom Ridolfi will have it that he caught a certain sweetness peculiar to the earlier works of that great master. Such is the Last Supper at S. Maria *Mater Domini*, and the Virgin at S. Stefano of Vicenza, executed in the very sweetest style, and esteemed one of his happiest performances. The great Carrara collection, as given in the work of Count Tassi, (page 88,) affords many specimens of both the above styles. Finally, in certain others, according to Zanetti, he displays greater powers of originality; as in the Epiphany in the island of S. Helena, where indeed we recognize one who copies nature accurately, but only the obvious nature; while he displays equal care in the disposition of his drapery, and in conforming his composition to the most approved rules. His works are for the most part characterized by a degree of diligence, an exquisiteness of finish, and an intimate blending of the colours, that sometimes renders us unable to trace his pencil: it is asserted by one of his biographers, that he spent a great deal of time on each of his pictures, and was always a long while in retouching them. In the unsparing application of his colours, as well as in many other particulars, he resembles Lotto; and though he has not the animation and sublimity of that master, yet, generally speaking, he perhaps exhibits more beauty in the heads of his female and infantine figures. Some are of opinion, that in certain of his heads he has presented us with the features of his daughter Violante, of whom Titian was deeply enamoured, and a portrait of whom, by the hand of her father, was to be seen in the collection of a Florentine gentleman named Sera, who purchased many rarities at Venice, both for the house of Medici and for himself—(Boschini, page 368.) Italy every where abounds with cabinet pictures ascribed to Palma; it abounds also with portraits, one of which has been lauded to the skies by Vasari; it abounds, too, with his Madonnas, accompanied for the most part by various Saints, in pictures of an oblong shape—a practice common to many other artists of that age.

But the crowd of connoisseurs, who are unacquainted even with the names of these artists, no sooner fall in with a picture holding a middle course between the dryness of Giovanni Bellini's, and the soft, well-fed pencilling of Titian's style, than they at once pronounce it to be a Palma; especially where they meet with well-rounded and well-coloured heads, well-finished landscapes, and drapery of a cream, rather than of a ruddy hue. Thus Palma is in every body's mouth; while the others, and these by no means few in number, are never once thought of, except when they happen to have subscribed their pictures with their names.

CARIANI.

One of those whose style bears a strong resemblance to that of Palma and Lotto, is Giovanni Cariani, an artist scarcely known beyond the limits of Bergamo and one or two of the neighbouring cities, and of whom Vasari makes no mention whatever. At Milan I met with a picture of his, bearing the date of 1514, and representing the Virgin surrounded by various Saints, where he seems to have taken Giorgione exclusively for his model. It is, if I mistake not, one of his juvenile performances, exhibiting figures of very inferior design compared with certain others of his which I have observed at Bergamo. Among them all, however, that which ranks first, is the picture of the Virgin at the throne, attended by a company of Saints and a glory of Angels, with other angels making melody at her feet. This is a most delightful picture, rendered still more charming by a beautiful landscape with little figures in the distance; exhibiting, too, a freshness of colouring and a fulness of pencilling, equal to that of the most studied works of the two Bergamasque painters already noticed; in conjunction with whom, indeed, he forms a triumvirate that might do honour to any city. Tassi relates that the celebrated Zanetti never visited Bergamo without gratifying himself with a sight of this picture; eulogizing it as the best altar-piece in the city, and one of the most beautiful that he had ever beheld. Cariani was moreover an excellent portrait painter, as is manifest from a picture in the possession of the Counts Albani, containing various portraits of that noble family; where, though confronted with the most eminent colourists he would almost appear the only one deserving of particular admiration.

PARIS BORDONE.

Paris Bordone, descended from a noble family of Trevigi, and endowed with a loftiness of genius corresponding with his birth, was for a short time a scholar of Titian's, then an ardent follower of Giorgione's, and lastly, the inventor of an original style whose peculiar gracefulness has never been imitated. There is in his pictures a gaiety and cheerfulness of colouring, which, as he could not make it truer than that of Titian, he seems to have been resolved to make more varied and more bewitching: while, at the same time, his paintings are by no means deficient in design, gracefulness of drapery, vivacity of countenance, or character of composition. At S. Giobbe he painted a St. Andrew raised to his cross, with an angel hovering over him, and rendering on him the crown of martyrdom; and having to introduce two other Saints, (St. Peter being one of them,) he represented the latter in the act of looking up to the martyr and in some sort envying him—an expedient equally novel and picturesque. The same observation holds good of his other works, many of which were executed for his native place or for the neighbouring towns. Every one of his cele-

parts is odd in itself; and yet every one of them is handled in a novel manner. Such is that genuine Paradise in the church of All Saints at Treviso; and, in the cathedral of the same city, that representation of the mysteries of Christianity in an altar-piece divided into six groups, for the purpose, I suspect, of gratifying those who wished to have it so; in which groups he seems to have comprised within a small compass whatever there is of the pleasing, the graceful, and the beautiful in all his other works. Among the most celebrated pictures in Venice is that of the Fisherman restoring the Ring to the Doge; a picture whose soft beauty contrasts admirably with the boldness of Giorgione's Tempest, near which it is placed. It is embellished with beautiful architectural ornaments and a number of animated and well-arranged figures, pleasingly varied both in attitude and drapery; insomuch that Vasari pronounces it his happiest performance. His cabinet pictures are very highly esteemed. Many of his Madonnas are readily recognised by the uniformity of their features: the same remark applies also to his portraits, the drapery of which he disposes in the manner of Giorgione, and in which he displays no small talent for invention and fanciful embellishment. Being invited to the court of Francis II., he there acquitted himself in a manner that gained the approbation of that monarch and his successor, and ensured his own substantial benefit. He had a son, who strove to emulate him in the art; but from the picture of David in the church of S. Maria Formosa at Venice, we may guess how much he was inferior to him.

PORDENONE.

Finally, I include in this number Gio. Antonio Licinio, called also Sacchiense or Cuticello, (58); having been wounded in the hand by a brother, he renounced his family name, and took that of Regillo. In general, however, he is called Pordenone, from the place of his nativity, formerly a town, but now a city of Friuli. In that province, says Vasari, "there were in his days a vast number of painters who had attained to eminence without having ever visited either Florence or Rome . . . . but Pordenone was the rarest genius and the most celebrated among them all; surpassing the rest in the conception of his historical pieces, as well as in design, spirit, correctness of colouring, address in fresco-painting, quickness of execution, boldness of relief, and every other accomplishment of art." It is by no means certainly known whether he frequented the school of

Giorgione, as some have imagined. And still less so whether he was a fellow pupil of his and Titian's under Gio. Bellini, as Ridolfi supposed. The opinion referred to by Ridolfi appears to me the nearest to the truth; that Pordenone having, while still a youth, studied the works of Pellegrino at Udine, subsequently adopted Giorgione's manner; following in this the bent of his own inclination—the painter's surest guide in the selection of his style. The other followers of Giorgione caught their master's manner, some more, some less accurately; but Pordenone caught its spirit—a spirit than which it is not easy to find in the whole of the Venetian school, one of a more ardent, bold, and elevated character. In Lower Italy Pordenone is scarcely known except by name. The picture in the Borghese palace containing portraits of his own family, is the largest work of his that I have seen in those parts. Indeed, it is but rarely that we meet with historical pieces of his even elsewhere, such, for example, as that exquisite Resurrection of Lazarus in the possession of the Conti family at Brescia. Nor do we find many altar-pieces of his beyond the confines of Friuli, where there are several scattered about in different places, though not all of them equally well authenticated. The genuineness of those few that he executed at Pordenone cannot be called in question, because he has described

there is a little volume of memoirs. The collegiate church contains two of them; one of them a Holy Family with St. Christopher, executed in 1515, and beautifully coloured, but not altogether free from inaccuracy; the other executed in 1535, where, together with other Saints and a perspective, St. Mark is introduced in the act of consecrating a priest—a picture, according to the author, "sketched rather than finished," (*posto in opera non finito.*) A more finished specimen was an Annunciation of his in the church of S. Pier Martire at Udine; but this has since been retouched and spoiled. Some, however, prefer the altar-piece in S. Maria dell' Orto at Venice to all the rest. It is a S. Lorenzo Giustiniani surrounded by various other Saints; amongst whom is a St. John the Baptist, partly in a state of nudity, and designed with a degree of accuracy that might do credit to schools the most distinguished in the anatomical style; and a St. Augustine, who seems to stretch forth his hand from the picture—a play of perspective repeated by this artist in various other places. At Piacenza, too, where he had established himself, there is another very beautiful work—a picture representing the Nuptials of St. Catherine, on a dark ground, which serves to give a high degree of roundness to those figures, the more delicate of which are so remarkable for gracefulness, as those of St. Peter and

St. Paul, placed on the two sides, are for dignity of character. In the latter of them, as also in the S. Rocco at Pordenone, he has presented us with a portrait of himself.

He displayed most merit, however, in his fresco works, great part of which he executed in Friuli; and very many of them in towns and cities are no longer known to foreigners except as containing some picture of Pordenone's. Such are Ceneda, Valvasone, Villanova, Varmo, Polcenigo; in which places it is notorious he exercised his talent. Some few works of his still exist in the palace of the Council at Murano, and at Genoa in the Doria palace; some few also at Venice in the church of S. Rocco, and in the convent of S. Stefano; a considerable number, and these in high preservation, in the cathedral of Cremona, and in S. Maria di Campagna at Piacenza, where, in different collections, and on certain façades, some other remains of his are pointed out. In his fresco paintings he is not always equally studied and correct; especially in his native Friuli, where in his youth he painted a good deal and at a low price. He shows more taste in his male than in his female figures, his beau ideal of which he seems to have derived not unfrequently from certain originals of a robust rather than an elegant form—those of the neighbouring Carnia—where he is said to have met with his first love. Still in every performance of his we may invariably trace the workings of a vigorous fancy, at once fertile in ideas, as well as capable of varying and subdividing them, and of expressing the different passions of the mind,—a painter who meets the difficulties of art with fore-shortenings the most novel, perspectives the most elaborate, and a relief which makes his figures look as if ready to start from the canvass.

In Venice he seemed even to surpass himself. The emulation, or rather, the enmity subsisting between him and Titian, spurred him on night and day to fresh exertion, and sometimes even led him to take the precaution of arming himself while he painted; and it is the opinion of many, that Titian profited by this rivalry, just as Raphael profited by that which subsisted between him and Michael Angelo. In this case, also, the one excelled in grandeur, the other in gracefulness, of style; or, as Zanetti expresses it, in Titian we recognise more of nature than of manner, in Pordenone nature and manner seem to contend for the mastery. The fact, however, of his having been Titian's rival, does him no little honour, and, in the Venetian school, ensures him at least the second rank, and that at a period so fruitful in eminent artists. Nay, at that time he was not without his party, who preferred him even to Titian himself: for, as I have elsewhere observed, there is nothing that so excites the admiration of the many, as the powerful effect and the magic of chiaroscuro—an art in which he paved the way for Giorgione. Pordenone enjoyed the favour of Charles V., who raised him to the rank of cavalier: he was subsequently invited to the court of Hercules II., Duke of Ferrara, where he shortly afterwards died; not without suspicion of having been poisoned.

TITIAN.

It is high time that we pass to Titian of Venice; as the reader, perhaps, has long since been of opinion. I shall not, however, be able to answer his expectation as I could wish; for when we have once formed a very high idea of an artist, all that one can say about him seems not only to fall short of his merit, but even in some sort to degrade him. But if, in estimating the talents of different artists, a precise indication of the distinguishing merits of each individual be considered more to the purpose than mere indulgence in vague panegyric, I may adduce the opinion of an accomplished critic, who used to say, that Titian saw further into nature, and copied it more correctly than any one else; and may also add such another, that he was of all painters the greatest confidant of nature—a sort of universal master, who, in all that he undertook to treat, whether the human figure, the elements, landscapes, or any other subject, has contrived to invest them with the strictest character of truth. He inherited from nature a solidity, evenness, and sagacity of temper, which led him to affect the true rather than the novel and the specious—a kind of temper as necessary to the composition of a great painter as of a great writer.

The education which he received, first from Sebastiano Zuccati, a native either of the Valteline or of Trevigi, and next from Gio. Bellini, rendered him a careful and accurate observer of every object, however minute, that presents itself to the eye: insomuch that, when, having now arrived at man's estate, he took it into his head to emulate Albert Durer, and painted at Ferrara the Christ to whom the Pharisee is showing the piece of tribute money; he even surpassed that elaborate master in minuteness. In the figures which compose this picture, one might almost count the hairs of the head and of the hands, as well as distinguish the pores of the skin, and the images of objects formed on the retina of the eye: and yet the work loses nothing by this minuteness; for while, at a distance, Durer's pictures dwindle into comparative insignificance, and lose much of their effect, this of Titian's even seems to expand and impress upon us its grandeur. There is, however, no other work of his in this style; and we know that, while he was still a young man, he applied himself to the freer and more easy manner pursued by Giorgione, at first his fellow-scholar, afterwards his rival. Some few portraits, painted by Titian during this brief period, are hardly to be distinguished from those of Giorgione himself. I have said during this brief period, for but a short time elapsed before he hit upon a new style of his own, less luminous, less fiery, and less elevated, but possessing greater sweetness, and calculated to charm the spectator, not by novelty of effect, but by its genuine character of truth. The earliest work that we meet with in this his own peculiar style, is an Archangel Raphael with Tobias by his side, in the sacristy of S. Marziale, painted when he was thirty years of age; nor, if we take Ridolfi for our guide, did any great while intervene before he executed at the Scuola della Carità that picture of our Saviour which is one of the noblest, and, as regards the number of figures, one of the richest works of his that now exists; many having perished in different conflagrations.

Design.—From these and other works painted by him in his best days, critics have formed their idea of his style; the question on which they are most divided being that of design. Mengs thinks that he can be placed among those who were eminent in design; setting him down as a painter of ordinary taste, and far from versed in the correct method of the ancients, though, had he studied it, he acknowledges he might have succeeded in it; seeing how true an eye he possessed for copying nature. In this opinion Vasari seems to coincide, where he introduces Michael Angelo after having looked at a Danae of Titian's, exclaiming, "that it was pity the Venetian artists were not taught to design accurately from the very first." Tintoretto, though he was his rival, pronounces a less unfavourable opinion, affirming that Titian "produced some things which it was impossible to surpass; but that some of his others might have been more correctly designed." Among the best he might well have placed—the Martyrdom of St. Peter in the church of St. John and St. Paul, in which, says Algarotti, the greatest masters have confessed "themselves unable to discover even the shadow of a defect,"—as well as the Bacchanal and the other pieces he executed for a cabinet of the Duke of Ferrara, which Agostino Caracci pronounces "to be the finest pictures in the world and the wonders of art." According to Du Fresnoy's opinion, he was less successful in the figures of men; but he adds, that "we meet with certain female and infantine figures of his that are exquisite both for design and colouring"—a compliment which, as regards the figures of his females, Algarotti also pays him, and, as regards those of children, even Mengs himself. Nay, it is a sort of received opinion that, in figures of this kind, no one ever equalled him; and that Poussin and Fiamingo, who attained such eminence in this branch of art, acquired it from Titian's pictures. Reynolds also affirms, that though his style is not altogether so chaste as that of certain others of the Italian schools, it is nevertheless accompanied by a sort of senatorial dignity; that in portrait painting his merits are of the highest order; and that, lastly, his works might be studied with advantage even by such as look for the sublime.

Zanetti assigns him the first rank in design among all the more distinguished colourists; he represents him as having attentively studied anatomy, and as having moreover copied the best remains of antiquity; but suggests that he never much cared to affect an intimate acquaintance with the muscles, nor always took the trouble to give ideal beauty to his contours; whether it was that he had not learnt the method of doing this sufficiently soon, or to whatever other cause we may attribute it. For the rest, he observes, "that Titian invariably exhibits an elegance, a correctness, and nobleness of character in his female and infantine figures; while for the most part he displays grandeur, condition, and dignity in those of his own;" and, in proof of his knowledge of anatomy, he produces the historical pieces painted in the sacristy of the church della Salute, where the beauty of the design is remarkable even in the extremities, and where its effect is moreover heightened by the intimate knowledge of foreshortening (*di sotto in su*) with which it is combined. Had the historian, however, taken into account the works of this artist scattered throughout different foreign countries, he might have added much more on the subject of his Bacchanals and his Venuses; one of which, in the Royal Gallery at Florence, was justly said to rival the Venus of Medicis, the last perfection of Grecian art. To prove his skill in the disposition of the drapery, Zanetti instances the St Peter painted over an altar of the Pesaro palace, with a mantle most ingeniously executed; adding, that he sometimes purposely neglected the drapery, in order to give bolder relief to some neighbouring object. Such being the discordant opinions entertained by profound connoisseurs, I shall not venture to interpose my own judgment. I will only observe, in praise of this accomplished artist, that had a more fortunate combination of circumstances led him to adopt more approved maxims of design, he would perhaps have been the first painter in the world. He would at any rate have made mankind unanimous in pronouncing him perfect in design, as they are already unanimous in pronouncing him to be perfect and altogether unrivalled in colouring.

Chiaroscuro and Colouring.—Numbers have treated of this latter, as well as of his chiaroscuro; among them, Zanetti, who spent so many years in examining it, handles it very copiously. Some of his remarks I have selected; observing, however, that Zanetti left it for the students to make a great many more reflections for themselves by actual inspection of Titian's works. And, in truth, his pictures are the surest guides we have to direct us in the right path as regards colouring; but they are like the writings of the classics, which, though equally open to all, and commented upon alike for all, afford instruction to those only who are capable of reflecting upon them. I have already noticed the brilliance which predominates in the works of the Venetian painters, and especially in those of Titian, whom the rest adopted as their model. I have observed, that it was the result of a very light-coloured imprimitura, or ground, upon which each of the colours being laid on again and again, they produce at length the effect of a transparent veil, and render the tints no less mellow than bright. Nor did he proceed in a different manner in his stronger shadows, covering them afresh with colour when dry, constantly seeking to give them greater force, and imparting to them more warmth where they seem just merging into the middle tints. In his management of shadow he displayed great judgment, adopting a method which cannot be said to be a mere copy of the natural, inasmuch as it possesses a good deal of the ideal. In the parts of his figures exposed to view, he principally shuns masses of bold and strong shadow, though they are sometimes to be met with in nature. They tend to produce a stronger relief, but they detract from the softness of the fleshes. Titian, for the most part, affected strong lights, taking care to soften down the less prominent parts by various shades of middle tints; and then, drawing the other parts and the extremities with more boldness than is perhaps to be found in nature, he contrived to invest fictitious objects with a degree of life and fascination greater than we even find in real ones. Thus, in his portraits, he makes the stronger lights fall on the eyes, the nose, and the mouth, leaving the other parts in a sort of pleasing indistinctness, which adds much to the spirited air of his heads as well as to the general effect.

But as mere skilfulness in the art of heightening or diminishing shadow is not enough, unless it be combined with corresponding skilfulness of colouring, he in this respect also pursued an ideal method, which consisted in employing, in their proper places, either single tints taken directly from nature, or such artificial ones as produce the illusion required. On his pallet he used to keep but a few simple colours; but he had the tact to select such as would produce the most variety and contrast; and was also well acquainted with the limits to which this contrast might be carried, and the proper moment for having recourse to it. Hence it never betrays any thing like exaggeration; the varied colours that rise one above another in his paintings, have all the appearance of resulting from nature, and not as the effect of consummate art. A piece of white cloth near to a naked figure makes it look as if worked up with bright vermilion; while in fact he merely used terra rossa with a little lake colour in the outlines and extremities. A similar result is produced in his pictures by objects of a dark or sometimes even of a black hue, which, besides contributing to the relief of the adjacent colours, serve to give greater effect to the figures worked up, as was said, by means of almost insensible middle tints. It was a saying of his, handed down to us by Boschini, that whoever would become a painter should make himself thoroughly acquainted with the properties of three colours, white, red, and black; and that when about to paint flesh, should never flatter himself with the hope of succeeding at the first trial, but only by rubbing in different colours repeatedly;

I here subjoin a few observations by Mengs, who so profoundly analysed Titian's style. He calls him the first, after the revival of painting, who managed to avail himself of the ideal in the different colours of dress. Before his time all colours were used indiscriminately, and were laid on with the same gradations of light and shade. Titian discovered (unless we suppose Giorgione to have taught him) that red serves to approximate objects, yellow to retain the rays of light, while azure is of use in strong shadows: nor was he less intimately versed in colours of a more juicy nature (colori succosi): thus he could impart the same grace, clearness, and dignity of colouring, to his shades and middle tints, as to his stronger lights; as well as diversify, by great variety of middle tints, the different complexions and the different superficies of bodies. Nor did any one better know how to maintain the equilibrium of the three colours afore-mentioned, on which the harmony of pictures depends; an equilibrium difficult to be observed in practice, and to which Rubens, notwithstanding his skill in colouring, could never perfectly attain.

Invention and Composition.—In invention and composition, Titian betrays his usual character; never executing any thing without consulting nature. In the number of his figures he is somewhat frugal, and in grouping them displays a dexterity and care which he used to illustrate by the simile of a bunch of grapes, the many separate parts of which compose a whole, well rounded as to shape, divested of heaviness by means of the different spacings and varied by middle tints and chiaroscuro, accordingly as the light falls upon it more or less powerfully. No contrasts that wear a studied appearance are to be found in these compositions; no violence of action that is not necessary to the story; the actors, generally speaking, preserve a staid and dignified demeanour, as though each respected the group of which he forms a part. Whoever admires the tone of the Greek reliefs, where all is nature and propriety, will ever prefer the gravity of Titian's to the sprightliness of Paolo's and Tintoretto's compositions, of which we shall have to speak elsewhere. Not that he was unskilled in that contrast both of action and of actors, in which his countrymen afterwards so much delighted; but he reserved it for Bacchanals, for battle-pieces—in short, for subjects that demanded it.

Expression.—In portraying the human countenance, it seems to be agreed that he was without a rival; and to this talent he in great measure owed his success, inasmuch as it served to give him an introduction to various splendid courts; as that of Rome in the time of Paul III., and those of Vienna and Madrid in the time of Charles V. and of his sons. Vasari confesses, that in this branch of art he attained the highest eminence, and that he executed portraits of numberless individuals of his time, and those the most illustrious either for their rank or their learning. But he evinced no less talent in delineating the affections of the mind. The Murder of St. Peter the Martyr, at Venice, and that of a Votary of St. Anthony, in the college of that name at Padua, are scenes than which I know not whether the whole compass of painting affords any thing more calculated to excite horror by the ferocity of the assassins, or compassion by the resigned demeanour of the victims. In the same manner, the great picture at the Grazie at Milan, representing the putting the Crown of Thorns on our Saviour's head, is animated with an expression that enchants us.

Keeping and Decoration.—With regard to keeping also and erudition, he has left not a few examples worthy of imitation: thus in the above-mentioned picture of the Crown of Thorns, wishing to mark the precise period of the event, he introduced into the prætorium a bust of Tiberius; a happy idea that might have done credit to a Raphael or a Poussin. In his architectural ornaments he sometimes availed himself of the assistance of others, especially that of the Rosa, of Brescia; yet his perspectives—that of the Presentation, for example—are very beautiful. In his landscape he is unrivalled; though he took care not to introduce them merely for the sake of ornament, like certain others, who, aware of their ability in this respect, have well-nigh made cypresses spring up out of the midst of the sea. Titian makes the landscape of a picture subordinate to the story, as in the case of the Murder of St. Peter the Martyr, where the gloom of the forest adds so much to the horrors of the scene; or else makes it contribute to give his figures greater effect, as in those pieces where the landscape is thrown into the distance. With what spirit and truth he represented the various effects of light, may be witnessed in his Martyrdom of S. Lorenzo in the church of the Jesuits at Venice, where he expressed in a manner so different the brightness of the fire, the flaring of the torches, and the splendour of a supernatural light which descends upon the Martyr,—a picture which has sustained great injury from time, but of which there is a sort of duplicate in the Escurial. He was also peculiarly happy in expressing the precise time of day when the incident, proposed to be represented, occurred; frequently making choice of the period about sunset, and drawing from it the most beautiful accidents of light.

Chiaroscuro of Titian.—From all that has been said we may infer, that Titian was not one of that class of Venetians who preferred rapidity of exe-

nor in regard to depth and accuracy of composition; although we must be cautious how we deny him even the attribute of rapidity. That he had a ready hand there can be no doubt; and of this, without prejudice to his design, he gave proofs in the fresco paintings which still exist at Feltre, and which in some measure compensate the loss of those executed in the capital; where there no longer remains any thing of this sort in tolerable preservation except a St. Christopher in the Ducal palace—a stupendous picture for character and expression. We must not look for the same facility of execution in his oil paintings. Indeed, he made no great pretension to it, and took great pains to attain to a perfect conception of his subject: nay, when he had once sketched his works with some degree of freedom and boldness, he laid them aside for a time in this condition, returning to them afterwards afresh with an eye prepared to purge them from every defect. Amidst a valuable collection of his finished pieces, the Barbarigo palace contains a few of these sketches. In the finishing of his works it is well known that he took great pains, and that he was at the same time very solicitous to conceal this circumstance: in fact, in some things of his we now and then meet with certain strokes of the pencil, so bold and spirited, that they enchant the professor; at once compassing a point long aimed at, and imparting to every object the genuine character of nature. Such was the method he pursued in his best days; but towards the close of his life, which the plague put an end to when he was now within one year of having attained the age of a hundred, his sight and hands failing him, he gave into a less finished style, executing his pictures by separate strokes of the pencil, and with difficulty making the colours blend together. Vasari, who saw him again in 1566, even at that period could no longer recognise Titian in Titian; and still more would this have been the case during the subsequent years of his life. Titian, however, with a weakness peculiar to old age, was not aware of this deterioration, and did not refuse to receive orders up to the very last year of his life. At S. Salvatore there is an Annunciation of his, in which there is nothing to arrest the spectator's attention except the great name of the author; and because some persons had asserted that it either was not, or at least did not appear to be his, he felt irritated at it, and with a sort of doting indignation affixed to it the following inscription: "Titianus fecit fecit." It is agreed, however, among those best able to give an opinion on the subject, that much may be learnt even from his latest works; just as Longinus, when speaking of the Odyssey, pronounces it indeed to be the production of old age, but still the production of a Homer. Some of the pictures of this latter period that we meet with in different collections, are considered doubtful; as are also certain copies executed by his disciples and retouched by him; particularly certain Madonnas and Magdalenes which I have seen in very many places, and with little or no variation in them. On this head we must not forget the story told by Ridolfi; that Titian, whenever he went from home, used purposely to leave the door of his studio open, in order that his scholars might surreptitiously copy the pictures he had left there; and that, after a while, finding these copies saleable, he gladly purchased them, and having bestowed a little pains in retouching them, caused them to pass for originals of his own. To this account the same historian adds the following marginal note:—*Vedi che accortezza!* "Observe what shrewdness!" To which I would add another:—"Remember that Titian's merit must not be estimated, as is sometimes the case, by duplicates of this sort."

Titian had not the same merit as a master, that he had as a painter. Whether it was from impatience of that irksomeness which accompanies the task of teaching, or whether it was rather from the fear of seeing a rival start up, he was always averse to giving instruction. He invariably treated with harshness, and even went so far as to persecute, Paris Bordone, who was possessed with an ardent desire of imitating him; Tintoretto he expelled from his studio; and his own brother, who had evinced an uncommon talent for painting, he dexterously turned to mercantile pursuits. "Hence," (says Vasari,) "there are but few who can, strictly speaking, be called his scholars, for he taught but little; every one, however, has made more or less proficiency according as he has known how to avail himself of Titian's performances."*

SCHIAVONE.

Andrea Schiavone, of Sebenico, surnamed Medula, may be ranked among the followers of Titian as regards his colouring, though even in this he displayed a certain original vivacity. Few have inherited from nature so decided a turn for painting; and of this it is said his father became aware,

* One of Titian's most successful followers was Bordone, of Treviso. "In Bordone's time," (says Lanzi,) "it was not usual at Venice, nor is it usual even now, [illegible]

when, on showing him over the city, whither he had taken him while yet a boy for the purpose of procuring him some situation, he found it difficult to get him from the spot wherever he chanced to meet with painters at work, and hence he procured him employment among them. Fortune, however, frowned upon him, and such was his poverty, that he was under the necessity of earning his daily subsistence rather as a menial than as an artist. Hence he began to paint without having grounded himself in design; nor had he for several years any other patrons than here and there a master-plasterer, who recommended him for the ornamenting of façades, or a master-painter of furniture, who availed himself of his assistance. Titian brought him into some notice by proposing him, among various other painters, for the Library of St. Mark, where he wrought with greater accuracy than perhaps any where else. Tintoretto, too, did justice to his merit; frequently assisting him in his works for the purpose of observing the art with which he coloured; and even keeping a specimen of his pictures in his own studio, being accustomed to say, that every painter should have done the same, but that he would have done wrong had he not designed better than Schiavone. Nay more, he even went so far as to imitate him; and at the Carmine executed an altar-piece on the subject of the Circumcision, so closely resembling his style, that Vasari actually described it as a work of Schiavone's. This artist, indeed, held Schiavone in such contempt as to assert, "that it was only by chance he now and then produced a good picture;" a charge indignantly repelled by Agostino Carracci, as may be seen in Bellori's life of Franco. In truth, with the exception of design, every thing else in Schiavone was highly deserving of commendation, whether we consider the beauty of the composition; the vivacity of the attitudes, copied from engravings of Parmigianino's works; the charms of the colouring, which possesses something of Andrea del Sarto's sweetness; or the style of pencilling, which is that of a consummate master. His reputation increased after his death; and his pictures, for the most part of a mythological character, were cut out from the pieces of furniture on which they were painted, and found their way into different collections. Guarienti cites three of these in the Dresden gallery; Rosa, four in the Imperial gallery at Vienna. I have met with some very charming ones of this sort in the Casa Pisani at S. Stefano, and in almost every other collection at Venice. At Rimini also, in the possession of the Padri Teatini, I saw two pictures of his that were made to match—a Nativity of our Saviour, and an Assumption of the Virgin —the figures of which are small, after the manner of Poussin, and among the most beautiful he ever executed.*

TINTORETTO.

James Robusti, the son of a Venetian dyer, and surnamed Tintoretto, was a scholar of Titian's, who, out of jealousy at his abilities, soon dismissed him from his studio. It was by no means Tintoretto's aim to be called a follower of Titian; on the contrary, he panted to become the head and founder of a new school, which should perfect Titian's manner, and add to it other merits in which it was deficient,—a noble idea, the offspring of a genius no less bold than fervid and sublime, whose ardour was rather increased than diminished by his dismissal from Titian's studio. Necessitated by his poverty to content himself with an incommodious apartment, he ennobled it with his earliest performances. In it he had affixed the following inscription:—"Michael Angelo's design

* About this time there flourished at Brescia—Alessandro Bonvicino, commonly called Il Moretto di Brescia—Il Romanino, inferior to the former according to Vasari, but equal to him in the opinion of Ridolfi—and Lattanzio Gambara, the scholar and son-in-law of Romanino.

and Titian's colouring;"—and as he copied the works of the latter with indefatigable industry, so he night and day studied casts taken from the antique and the statues at Florence, to which he added many ancient statues and reliefs. In a catalogue of ancient sculpture of the year 1582, cited by Morelli, we find mention of a head of Vitellius, which Tintoretto "was constantly copying and designing." He used frequently to design from models by candle-light, the better to produce strong shadows, and thus acquire facility in the representation of powerful chiaroscuro. With the same view he made wax or clay models, and having taken care to drape them properly, arranged them in little houses made of card or pieces of wood, so contrived as to exhibit correctly the effects of light and shade. These same models he also suspended from the ceiling by pieces of string, placing them in various positions, and drawing them in different points of view in order to make himself master of the art of foreshortening on ceilings—an art in which at that time the Venetians were less intimately versed than the Lombard painters. Meanwhile, he did not neglect the study of anatomy, seeking to make himself thoroughly acquainted with the action of the muscles and the structure of the human frame; and taking the utmost pains to represent the naked figure under various foreshortenings and in diffirent attitudes, in order to impart to his compositions all the variety that we meet with in nature. By such pursuits as these he prepared the way for the introduction of the right mode of study among his followers, which consists in beginning by designing the best models, and, after having thus acquired an idea of a correct style, proceeding to copy the naked figure and amend its defects. With these helps he united a genius which Vasari, though one of his severest critics, could not help admiring, pronouncing it the most terrible (il più terribile) the art had ever witnessed ;—an imagination always fertile in new ideas; a fire and animation which enabled him to conceive correctly the boldest characters the passions can assume, and which never failed him till he had completely transferred them to the canvass.

But what are great erudition and transcendent genius, or what are all the other requisite accomplishments of an artist put together, without diligence, a virtue which, according to Cicero, in itself comprises all the rest? This virtue Tintoretto for some time possessed, and he then produced works in which the severest critics could not find the shadow of a fault. Of this kind is the Miracle of the Slave at the school of St. Mark, which he painted in his thirty-sixth year, and which passes for one of the wonders of Venetian painting. Here the colouring is in Titian's style, the chiar-

colours remarkably bold, the composition close and correct, the figures select, the drapery studied, the attitudes of the bystanders incredibly diversified, appropriate, and animated; more especially that of the Saint who flies to administer relief, and which presents us in some sort with the lightness of a disembodied spirit. There, too, he painted some other pieces of such exquisite beauty, that, on beholding them, Pietro da Cortona exclaimed: —"Were I to take up my abode in Venice, not a festival should pass by without seeing me resort hither to feast my eyes on these objects, and, above all, on the design." The Crucifixion at the school of S. Rocco—than which, notwithstanding the hackneyed nature of the subject, it is impossible to meet with any thing treated in a more novel manner—is also a highly esteemed performance. Nor are there wanting other examples of his extraordinary powers in that place, which he filled with pictures as remarkable for their variety and novelty; but, for the sake of brevity, I shall content myself with naming, as a third, the Last Supper, which is now in the church della Salute; having been removed from the refectory of the Crociferi, for which it was executed. Those who saw it in the situation for which it was intended, have described it as a miracle of art; for the construction of the room was so well followed up in the picture, and imitated with such skilfulness of perspecchio, that it made the apartment look double its real size. Nor are these three works, on which he inscribed his name, as being those on which he chiefly prided himself, the only ones worthy of his great reputation: Zanetti records not a few others finished with exquisite care, and all to be seen in public at Venice; to say nothing of those that are scattered through other cities of Europe.

But diligence is rarely found to accompany a rage for achieving a great deal—the true source in this and a multitude of other artists of painting badly, or at least worse than they might have done. Hence Annibal Caracci has remarked, that in many of his pictures Tintoretto appeared inferior to Tintoretto; and Paul Veronese, though so great an admirer of his genius, used to complain "that he did injury to his fellow-artists by thus painting in any style, which was in fact the very way to lower the respectability of the profession." (Ridolfi.) Similar exceptions may be taken to that numerous class of his works, which, invented on the spur of the moment, executed without study, and in great part left unfinished, betray both error of design and defect of judgment. In these we sometimes meet with a crowd of figures either superfluous or badly grouped; and, what is still more usual, all of them in a state of violent exertion, without a single spectator quietly looking on, as in the case of Titian's works and those of others who excelled in composition. In Tintoretto's figures we must not look for that senatorial dignity which Reynolds found in those of Titian. Tintoretto aimed at sprightliness rather than decorum, and from among the common people of his native place, who are perhaps the sprightliest of Italy, he derived the models both of his heads and his attitudes; and applied them sometimes even to the gravest subjects. In some of his Last Suppers, we now and then meet with an Apostle that reminds us of the gondoliers of the grand canal, when, with body bent forward and one arm lifted up to ply the oar, they raise the head with a certain air of [illegible] levity, either for the purpose of keeping on the look out, of exchanging repartees, or engaging in disputation. He also deviated from Titian's method of colouring; making use of dark grounds instead of such as were of a white chalky colour; a circumstance from which his pictures have suffered more than any others in Venice. Nor is the choice or general tone of his colours the same as Titian's; the azure, or ash-coloured, is that which predominates; and this detracts from the glory of the picture, as much as it aids the effect of the chiaroscuro. In his bodies, those of his portraits more especially, we often meet with a sort of vinous tinge. Even the proportions of his figures are different from those of Titian; he does not affect the fulness of the letters; aiming rather at lightness, and sometimes erring on the side of slenderness. The most neglected parts of his works, however, are the draperies: most of them displaying either long and straight folds, or too much airiness, or some other kind of mannerism. Of his want of judgment, or rather his pictorial extravagances, it were useless to say any thing, Vasari having already said more than enough while giving a description of his Last Judgment at S. Maria del Orto.

Yet Vasari, notwithstanding the severity of his criticism, was forced to confess, that if in that picture, (and the same is true of others,) its author had paid so much attention to the several parts as he did to the whole piece, it would have been a most stupendous work. Even in those pieces in which, if we may so say, he took it into his head to play the improvvisatore, he still shows a command of pencil worthy a first-rate master; a certain originality of genius which here and there manifests itself in the play of light, the difficult foreshortenings, the fanciful invention, the relief, and harmony of his performances; and, where we chance to meet with them in good preservation, even in the gracefulness of his colouring. In the art of animating his figures, more especially, he proves himself a consummate master; it being an observation so common as almost to have passed into a proverb, that Tintoretto is the one to study

its movement throughout. On this head Pietro da Cortona used to remark, that were we to inspect every picture that has yet been engraved, we should meet with no artist to equal him in fire and animation, (furore pittoresco.) He lived to a great age, painting continually, so as almost to make it impossible to give a complete catalogue of his works; seeking every means in his power to give vent to his irrepressible ardour either in pictures of so extraordinary size, or such at least as were crowded with actors; amongst which, the Paradise, in the hall of the Great Council, painted in old age, and peopled with an almost countless multitude of figures, extorted the praise and admiration even of the Carracci themselves. Had those figures been disposed more judiciously, and grouped in a less confused manner, Algarotti would not have censured this picture as he did, nor have adduced it as an instance of crude composition. Genuine works of Tintoretto's are not to be found in any great number in the galleries of Italy. In Venice, however, they are by no means rare, and there we may by actual inspection satisfy ourselves of the truth of that remark which, when we simply read it in Ridolfi, appears so improbable—that Tintoretto finished his performances with all the nicety of a miniature painter. The Barbarigo palace at S. Polo contains a Susanna of his of this character, where in a small space he has represented a park, with birds and rabbits, and every thing else that can delight the eye, the whole as exquisitely finished as the figures themselves.

Little need be said of his scholars, of whom none succeeded better than Domenico Tintoretto, his son. Domenico followed his father's footsteps, but only as Ascanius followed those of Æneas—that is to say, "non passibus æquis." In the heads, the colouring, and arrangement of his pieces, he strongly resembles his father; but in point of genius he is greatly inferior to him; and some of his more spirited works are either referred at once to the latter, or he at least is suspected to have contributed the more meritorious parts.

BASSANO.

Jacopo da Ponte, son of Francesco da Ponte, was born at Bassano, a short time after the birth of Tintoretto, and was instructed by his father in the rudiments of art. The earliest works that he executed in his native place, at the church of S. Bernardino, bear the impress of such an education. Repairing afterwards to Venice, he was recommended to Bonifacio, a master so jealous of his art than was Titian or Tintoretto; insomuch that Bassano never had an opportunity of seeing him lay on his colours, except by peeping through the holes in the door of his studio." At Venice he abode a short time, exercising himself in designing the sketches of Parmigianino, and in copying the pictures of Bonifazio and Titian, whose scholar he was according to some manuscripts. And if conformity of manner (which is but a very equivocal proof) were sufficient ground to go upon, we should be compelled to believe this; so much does Bassano's second style resemble that of Titian. There are but few pictures in this style to be met with in his native place: as a Flight into Egypt at S. Girolamo, and a Nativity of Christ in the possession of a Dr. Larber; both of these juvenile productions, but such that they might at the time have seemed to hold out the promise of another Titian; so much have they of the same loveliness of manner.

The death of his father obliged Jacopo to return and fix himself in his native place, at the present day a rich and populous city, and even then by no means a contemptible spot, delightfully situated, abounding with flocks and herds, and lying conveniently for markets and fairs. From circumstances such as these arose by little and little that third style of his which is nature, grace, and simplicity itself, and which in Italy served to a prelude to that adopted by a whole nation of foreigners—the Flemings. In his painting Barocci pursued two different methods. The first exhibits high finish and exquisite union of colours, combined with freedom of touch; the second (to which there are no means of attaining except by passing through the first) consists of pleasing and lucid tints laid on by separate strokes of the pencil, and with a command of hand and fearlessness of manner, that, when closely examined, makes the picture look like a confused mass of colouring, but at a distance produces a most agreeable and magical effect. In each of these he evinces an originality of style, which in great part consists in a certain lucidness of composition. This composition partakes at once of the triangular and the circular; aiming at a certain contrast of attitude, so that if one figure is seen in face, the other is made to turn its back on the spectator; and yet seeking to preserve a sort of analogy, so that various heads, or, in default of these, some other figure may be found in the same line. With regard to the management of light, he makes it fall in partial masses without much diffusion, but displays consummate skill in causing it to combine to the harmony of the whole; for by means of this paucity of light, aided by the frequency of middle tints and the sparing use of blacks, he admirably contrives to blend the most opposite colours.

In giving gradation to his lights, he often makes the shade of an inner figure serve as a ground to one more forward, causing but little light to fall upon them, but that of a very bold and vivid character at their angles; as on the top of the shoulders, on the knees, and the elbows: to which end he adjusts his draperies in a manner natural in appearance, but in fact adapted with exquisite art to the furtherance of the system; varying their folds according to the difference of their materials, and that with a delicacy of tact that falls to the lot of few. His colours sparkle like gems, especially his greens, which possess an emerald tinge peculiar to himself.

At the outset of his career, Jacopo aspired to boldness of style, and evinced some propensity for it in certain pictures on the façade of the Casa Michieli which still exist: of these, the most extolled is a Samson slaying the Philistines; works that partake of the boldness of Michael Angelo's manner. But, whether it was that he followed the natural bent of his genius, or merely his better judgment, he afterwards confined himself to smaller proportions and subjects of less force. Even in his altar-pieces the figures are usually much less than life, and never very animated; insomuch that it has been said that, with Tintoretto even old men assume the sprightliness of youth, while with Bassano even young men put on the dullness of age.

In his pictures we meet not with those splendid architectural ornaments which give such an air of stateliness to the compositions of the Venetian school; he seems to make a point of selecting subjects favourable to the introduction of candle-lights, huts, landscapes, cattle, brazen utensils; objects which he had continually before his eyes, and which he copied with surprising accuracy. His ideas were somewhat confined, and hence he was apt to repeat them; a fault in some measure attributable to his situation,—it being an indisputable fact, that the ideas both of artists and writers become expanded and multiplied in large cities, while in small towns they become contracted. All this may we observe in his cabinet pictures, which were the most usual occupation of his life; for he did not produce many large altar-pieces. He worked at them at his leisure in his studio, and with the assistance of his scholars prepared a considerable quantity of different sizes: he then despatched them to Venice, and sometimes to the more frequented fairs; whence so great is the number of *Bassanos*, that in good collections it is rather a disgrace to want them than an honour to be possessed of them. In these the same subjects continually recur—facts borrowed from the Old and New Testament—Feasts of Martha, the Pharisee, or the Rich Man, with a prodigal display of brazen utensils—Noah's Ark, the Return of Ja-

tells the Angel announcing the glad Tidings of Salvation to the Shepherds, pictures which all of them exhibit a multitude of different animals—the Queen of Sheba, or the Three Wise Men, with a princely parade of velvets and rich cloths—the Burying of our Saviour, or the Placing of his Body in the Tomb, by torchlight. His pictures, when they treat of profane subjects, represent at one time cattle or brazen utensils exposed for sale; at another, the various occupations of husbandry corresponding with the four seasons of the year; at another, smiling human figures, a kitchen service, a poultry yard, or similar objects. Not only do the same stories, however, and the same compositions return upon us in every collection, but even the same faces, which he was apt to copy from those of his own family; employing one of his own daughters for instance, at one time as a Queen of Sheba, at another as a Magdalene, at another as a Country-girl carrying fowls to the cage. I have even seen entire pictures, sometimes in small, sometimes in large proportions, bearing the name of "Bassano's Family." Of the former kind I noticed one in Genoa in the possession of the Sig. Ambrogio Durazzo, where were represented the painter's daughters intent on feminine occupations, an infant son at play, and a servant maid in the act of lighting a candle. Of the latter kind there is one in the Medicean Museum, representing a company of musicians.

By this means he virtually confessed the poverty of his imagination, but he derived from it one important advantage: it was this, that by dint of repeating the same subjects over and over again, he brought them to the utmost degree of perfection he was capable of imparting to them. Such was the case in the Nativity of Christ, placed in the church of S. Giuseppe at Bassano; the masterpiece not only of Jacopo, but I had almost said of modern painting itself, as far as regards force of colouring and chiaroscuro. Such too was the case with the Burial of Christ at the Seminario of Padua, which Madame Patin caused to be engraved amongst the "Immagini de' celebri Dipintori," because she had never met with any other that breathed such a spirit of piety and holy horror. Such, lastly, was the case with the Sacrifice of Noah at S. M. Maggiore of Venice, in which he collected in one view all the beasts and birds that he had scattered through his other works; a picture so much admired by Titian himself, that he was desirous of purchasing a copy of it for his own studio.

Hence it happens that those works of Bassano, which he executed at a certain age and with care, are in very great repute and fetch very high prices.

though they are not exempt from certain defects of perspective, certain impropriety of attitude, and certain errors of composition, especially in point of symmetry; it being a very common remark, that he was but little versed in drawing the extremities; whence he did his utmost to avoid the introduction of hands and feet into his pictures. These charges, and others already noticed, may admit of extenuation; there being works of Bassano's which prove that, when he so pleased, he could acquit himself much better than he was wont to do. That he knew how to vary his composition we may infer from the Nativity in the Ambrosian Library at Milan; and in the same manner he might have varied others. That he was capable of conceiving both with propriety and novelty, we may gather from his S. Rocco at Vicenza; and the same he might have done in other cases. That he knew how to draw the extremities with accuracy, we learn from his S. Peter, in the church of the Umiltà at Venice. That he knew how to impart an air of dignity to his heads, is evident from a picture of the Queen of Sheba that I met with at Brescia; and this he might have done in other instances. But whether it was that he found the task too irksome, or from whatever other cause, he rarely attempted any thing of this kind; contenting himself with having attained the highest pitch of excellence in his own peculiar method of colouring, illuminating, and shading his pictures. And so universally was he admired, that he received numberless orders from various courts, and even an invitation to become painter to that of Vienna. What is more, Bassano, notwithstanding his defects, was honoured with the highest commendations, though not by Vasari, yet by other painters of greater name; by Titian, as we have already observed; by Annibal Caracci, who was so completely deceived by a book of his painted on a table, that he stretched out his hand to take it up, as though it had been a real one; and by Tintoretto, who had a high opinion of his colouring, and in some respects strove to imitate it.

Bassano brought up his four sons to the same profession, and by them his method was communicated to others, so that the Bassanese school lasted about a century, though all the while declining and departing from its primitive splendour. Of the members of Jacopo's family, the two who evinced the most aptitude for imitating him were Francesco and Leandro; and he used to pride himself on the former for the inventive powers he displayed, on the latter for his extraordinary talent at portrait painting. Of the two others, Giambatista and Girolamo, he used to say, that they were excellent copyists of his works. All these, but especially the two last, having been initiated by their father in those branches of art which he himself practised, have imitated his manner so exactly, that many of their copies, executed both during their father's lifetime and after his death, have ever since that period imposed upon purchasers, and passed for originals of Jacopo.

PAOLO CALIARI,

COMMONLY CALLED

PAOLO VERONESE.

WHILE the Bassanese painters were employing themselves in portraying the simplest objects of rural nature in pictures of a small size, another school sprung up at Verona, which surpassed all others in representing, in pictures on a very large scale, all the most beautiful objects of art, architectural ornaments, rich dresses, and other costly decorations, together with splendid retinues of servants and a degree of pageantry worthy of royalty itself. It still remained to bring this branch of art to perfection; and it is the glory of Paolo Caliari that he accomplished it. He was the son of one Gabriello, a sculptor of Verona, and being destined by his father for the same pursuit, was accordingly instructed in the art of design and of modelling in wax. The youth, however, having evinced an extraordinary predilection for painting, his father placed him under the tuition of Badile, with whom, in a short time, he made astonishing progress. He had, however, fallen on an age in which, to arrive at distinction, great exertion was indispensable; so fertile was the Veronese school in men of talent.

Those who took the lead there when Paolo began to come into notice, were three fellow-citizens, whose names, in their native place, are, I had almost said, in as high repute as that of Paolo himself;—Batista d'Angelo, surnamed il Moro; Domenico Ricci, surnamed il Brusasorci; and Paolo Farinato, called degli Uberti. These three were invited to Mantua by the Cardinal Ercole Gonzaga to paint each of them an altar-piece in the cathedral; and with them Paolo also was invited, who, though younger than either, in the opinion of Vasari and Ridolfi, surpassed them all in this trial of skill.

Paolo Caliari found the public prepossessed in favour of the above-mentioned artists, and in his native place attracted but very little notice during his earlier years. The public, always slow to appreciate rising talent, either knew not, or did not believe, that he had surpassed all his competitors at Mantua; so that the youth, urged by want, quitted Verona, having behind him, even an altar at S. Fermo, a Madonna between two Saints, with some few other first-fruits of his genius. He repaired at first to Vicenza, and afterwards to Venice. Nature had endowed him with a genius for the noble, the elevated, the magnificent, the pleasing, and the vast; nor was any provincial city capable, like Venice, of furnishing him with ideas proportioned to his powers. There he set about improving his colouring after the methods of Titian and Tintoretto; but seems to have aimed at surpassing them in the elegance and variety of his decorations; whence his admirers were wont to assert that, even at that period, he used assiduously to study casts taken from ancient statues, as well as the engravings of Parmigianino's and Albert Durer's works. The first works that he produced at Venice, in the sacristy of S. Sebastiano, present us only with the first germs of his style, in the air of the heads, and the variety of drapery and attitude; for the rest, his manner was still somewhat timid, betraying rather a careful blending of the colours, than ease and boldness of pencilling. He wrought in a freer and more agreeable style a short time afterwards on the ceiling of the same church, where he represented the story of Esther,—a work which gained him the admiration of the public, and served to introduce him to the very honourable works to which he was employed by the senate.

Meanwhile, he had an opportunity of visiting Rome, whither he went in the suite of the ambassador Grimani, and where, at sight of the ancient and modern works of that city, "he felt his powers expand," (al volo sue senti crescer le penne,) as he afterwards gave proof in the Palazzo Pubblico at Venice. Here it is that he displays his love of decoration in every picture that he painted; but especially in that Apotheosis of Venice, where he has represented her seated on high, arrayed in royal robes, crowned by Glory, trumpeted by Fame, attended by Honour, Liberty, and Peace: Juno and Ceres are also introduced as personifications of Grandeur and Felicity. In the upper part of the picture we see magnificent architectural ornaments and colonnades; lower down, in a sort of gallery, we see a multitude of matrons with their sons, as well as a number of grandees in their robes of office; and still lower, warriors on horseback, arms, standards, prisoners, and trophies. This picture, or, to give it its true and specific name, this soffit, is a compendium of those wonders with which Paolo delights the eye, presenting us with a work that charms us no less as a whole than by the beauty of the component parts;—brilliant skies, sumptuous edifices, that seem to invite the feet of the spectator; heads both sprightly and dignified, chosen for the most part from nature, and embellished by art; airs heads at once graceful, expressive, and well contrasted; draperies of the most costly kind both for make and materials; colours, majesty, harmony, and a degree of magnificence worthy so august a subject; perspective that throws objects into distance without making them displeasing or when near; colours of the liveliest kind, sometimes separate, sometimes contrasted, blended with a degree of skill peculiar to himself, and such as no precepts could teach; a command of pencilling that combines the utmost rapidity with the deepest judgment, and in which every stroke is made to tell—accomplishments these which had then become familiar to him, and which constitute the distinguishing character of his genius.

Still, however, this work did not so much contribute to his celebrity as the Suppers he painted. It would be unpardonable in any one who undertakes to treat of his style, not to notice a subject which was more familiar to him than any other—a subject which he repeated so often, and of which, by dint of pencilling it and varying it in different ways, he made even the greatest princes ambitious of possessing specimens. Some of these I have met with on a small scale, and all of them beautiful—the Last Supper, in S. Sofia at Venice; another highly finished work on the same subject in the Borghese palace at Rome; the Feast given to the Poor by St. Gregory, in the possession of the Serviti of Vicenza; besides others in different collections. In Venice he painted four Suppers for the refectories of four religious establishments, all of them on a very large scale, and displaying great fertility of invention. The first of these, thirty palms in length, representing the Marriage of Cana, is still at S. Giorgio Maggiore: copies of this work have found their way into every part of the world; indeed, it is inestimable, both for the number of figures it contains, which amount to one hundred and thirty, and the portraits of princes and illustrious personages who lived at the time; and yet it brought its author only ninety ducats. The second, representing the Supper prepared by Matthew for our Saviour, in the church of St. John and St. Paul, is in better preservation, and is in high repute for the heads, all of which Paolo, at an advanced age, copied for his own studio. The third is at St. Sebastian's, and represents the feast of Simon. The fourth, on the same subject, which was in the refectory of the Servi, was sent to Louis XIV., king of France, and placed at Versailles: and this was by the Venetian artists preferred to all the rest; whence they have supplied us with many copies of it. Indeed, the author himself made a copy of it for the refectory of the monks of SS.

Nazario and Celso, which is now in the fine collection of the Doria palace at Genoa; and this, though of smaller dimensions, is considered equal to any of the preceding, and has been engraved by the celebrated Volpato. Another, on the same subject, was also sent from Venice to Genoa, and this I saw in the possession of the Durazzo family, together with a Magdalene, which may be called one of the wonders of art. In these pictures how wide a field was opened for the introduction of architectural ornaments, and how happily did Paolo avail himself of them to add to the spectacle of the feast! What varied passions has he expressed in the principal actors, and how appropriate to the time! How splendid are the decorations of the table, how choice the viands, how costly the dresses of the guests! Where there is so much beauty, we may well pardon some inaccuracies of design, into which Paolo occasionally falls, and some inattention to antique costume, of which he is guilty continually. At any rate we know that Guido, great as he was, overlooked these defects, inasmuch that he used to say,— "Were it given me to choose what painter I would be, I would be Paolo Veronese; in others we discover vestiges of art, but in him all is nature."

This painter, during the sixty years that he lived, produced a great number of works; but he cannot, like many others, be charged with having produced too many. Paolo did not execute a single picture but what was worthy of him; almost every one of them, observes Ridolfi, has found some copyist ready to repeat it; an honour that artists have not thought proper to pay to Tintoretto's works, or those of many others. The plan he pursued of using light grounds, and, as far as he was able, virgin tints, has contributed to the preservation and the freshness of his colouring. In Venice, we meet with pictures of his that are still radiant with all the beauties that he shed over them. One of the most celebrated is that in the Pisani palace, representing the Presentation of the family of Darius to Alexander the Great, which astonishes us by its magnificence, and moves us to pity by its expression. The Rape of Europa was formerly not less admired; a work which he executed on a large scale in various groups; imitating in this the Leda of Coreggio; in the first group, Europa appears amidst a company of Virgins in the act of caressing the Bull, and of attempting to mount upon his back: in the second, she is seen actually mounted, and riding delightedly along the shore, followed by the shouts of her companions: in the third, (the only one in large proportions,) she is seen borne over the waves, herself filled with terror, and her maidens vainly bewailing her loss.

This painting, which adorns the Ducal palace, having suffered much from time, has been retouched.

At Verona, the climate of which is more favourable to paintings, it is easier to meet with works of Paolo's unimpaired by restoration. Many of the nobles possess specimens of them, especially the Bevilacqua family, which formerly patronized him; and it was out of gratitude for this, that, in a portrait which he painted for one of the family, he introduced himself standing by in the character of a domestic. But his S. Giorgio, which some look upon as the best picture at Verona, is perhaps the least preserved work of his that now exists. The S. Giuliano of Rimini, another exquisite picture, and worthy almost of being compared with the S. Giorgio,—the S. Afra of Brescia,—and the S. Justina of Padua, which are in their respective churches, have suffered but little; but the last is placed too high. Paolo executed a great number of cabinet pictures. Portraits; Venuses, Adonises, Cupids, Nymphs, and figures of the like kind, in which he could indulge in elegance of form, fanciful embellishment, and novelty of invention, were the subjects most familiar to his pencil: these are to be met with in many different galleries; even in the Imperial one. Among sacred subjects, his favourite was that of the Espousals of St. Catherine, and of those one of the most studied found its way into the Royal collection at the Pitti palace. He also painted a good many Holy Families, in which he sought to avoid the more hacknied style of composition by introducing new conceits. Even his sacred pieces were many of them copious historical compositions; as, for instance, the Massacre of the Innocents in the Borghese palace, as exquisitely finished as though it had been an illumination; the Esther, belonging to the king of Sardinia, at Turin; the Queen of Sheba, (accompanied by a troop of maidens,) before the throne of Solomon. Saloons and other apartments, as well as various façades, embellished by fresco paintings of his, such as poetical allegories or historical pieces, are frequently to be seen both at Venice and in the palaces and villas of the Venetian state. One of these villas, in the territory of Asolo, which formerly belonged to the Doge Manin, is well worthy of a visit: the architecture is Palladio's, the stuccos Vittoria's, the pictures of the Muses, and those of various other pagan deities, are the works of Paolo—a combination of talent that might suffice to render this villa as famous among those of the moderns, as that of Lucullus was among those of the ancients.*

* The more distinguished of Paolo's school, were—Benedetto Caliari, his brother, and Carlo and Gabriele Caliari, his sons. Batista Zelotti was at once the imitator, the companion, and the rival of Paolo.

VENETIAN SCHOOL.

EPOCH III.

OWING TO THE MANNERISTS OF THE SEVENTEENTH CENTURY, PAINTING DECLINES AT VENICE.

It would seem the fated condition of all sublunary things, that they should never continue long in the same state, so that, after they have attained their highest elevation, we may shortly afterwards look for their decline. On no point whatever can the glory of pre-eminence be long confined to one single spot or one single nation. It is continually shifting from place to place: those who yesterday received laws from such or such a people, to-day impose them; and those who are to-day the teachers of a nation, will to-morrow be anxious to become its disciples. As regards painting, we have already witnessed these revolutions in the works of the Florentine and Roman schools, which, having attained their zenith, began to decline precisely at the time when that of Venice was rising into fame. We shall now have to witness the decline of this latter, at the very time when that of Flo-

school began to lift up its head once more, and when that of Bologna attained its highest eminence; and what is still more surprising, attained it by studying the works of the Venetian school. Thus it is! The Caracci studied the works of Titian, Giorgione, Paolo, and Tintoretto, and thence formed styles and reared pupils that did honour to the whole of the seventeenth century. The Venetians studied these same models, and derived from them a degree of mannerism which they themselves carried to a lamentable excess, but their disciples still more so. These, having turned their attention in the first instance to the works of the more classic artists, and attained some degree of skill in design and colouring, aimed at filling large pieces with figures not taken from nature, but derived either from the engravings and pictures of others, or from their own imagination; and always fancied they wrought the better, in proportion as they wrought the quicker. I cannot but think that the example set by Tintoretto was rather prejudicial than serviceable to that age. Few would give themselves the trouble to rival him in that deep knowledge of the art which serves in some measure to throw a veil over his defects. His haste, his negligence, his impetuosity, they imitated readily enough; and his great reputation served to cover their faults. The earliest of these, however, still mindful of the masters of a better age, did not rush into the same excesses as certain others: on the contrary, by the greater vivacity of their style, and its superior colouring, they acquitted themselves better than the mannerists of the Florentine and Roman schools. But to these there succeeded others, whose scholars went on deviating more and more from the methods of the old masters.

PALMA GIOVANE.

Jacopo Palma the younger, so called to distinguish him from his great-uncle, may, with equal propriety, be called the last painter of the golden age, and the first of the degenerate one. Born in 1544, and initiated in the rudiments of the art by Antonio his father, a painter of little merit, he proceeded to exercise himself in copying the works of Titian and the other more distinguished Venetians. When he had reached the age of fifteen, the Duke of Urbino took him under his protection, and carried him to his capital; and from thence he passed on to Rome, where he remained eight years. By this means he grounded himself thoroughly in his profession, designing the an-

mains of antiquity, copying the works of Michael Angelo and Raphael, and, above all, studying the chiaroscuros of Polidoro. This latter was his chosen model; next to him, his favourite was Tintoretto; for nature had predisposed him to impart to his figures the lightness and vivacity visible in theirs. Returning to Venice, he brought himself into notice by some works which he executed with care; and there are some professors who have lavished on these the highest encomiums, discovering in them the better maxims both of the Roman and Venetian schools. All his works are executed with a certain facility, which constitutes the distinguishing talent of this artist; but a talent no less dangerous in painting than in poetry. Notwithstanding his efforts to bring himself into vogue, he was but little employed: the post was already occupied by those consummate masters, Tintoretto and Paolo Veronese; and on them all the more lucrative orders devolved. Palma found means to introduce himself as a third, having by his obsequiousness gained over to his interest Vittoria, at that time in high repute, both as an architect and sculptor, and the arbiter even of those works on which painters themselves were employed. This Vittoria, chagrined at the little deference shown him by Tintoretto and Paolo, began to patronize Palma, and even to assist him with his advice; and thus brought him into notice.

No great while, however, elapsed, before Palma, now overwhelmed with orders, began to remit much of his former diligence. In process of time he became still more careless, when, his more aged competitors being now no more, and he himself freed from rivalry, he began to hold undisputed sway, and to despatch his works in a more hurried manner. His pictures might not unfrequently be called mere daubs. To induce him to execute a picture worthy of his reputation, it became necessary to give him whatever time he thought proper to require, and to pay him a price not measured by the opinion entertained of his merits by others, but by his own discretion; with which, to say the truth, he was by no means overstocked. It was thus that he painted for the noble family of Moro the beautiful picture of S. Benedetto in the church of SS. Cosmo and Damian; of the same stamp, indeed, he produced a good many others at Venice during his last days, and especially the celebrated naval battle of Francesco Bembo in the Palazzo Pubblico. Several highly esteemed performances of his are to be met with elsewhere, some of them noticed by Ridolfi, and others that were unknown to him; as the S. Apollonia at Cremona, the S. Ubaldo and the Nunziata at Pesaro, and the Discovery of the Cross at Urbino—a picture crowded with figures, and possessing great beauty, variety, and expression. His colours are fresh, soft, and transparent, not so gay as those of Paolo, but gayer than those of Tintoretto; and though laid on somewhat sparingly, yet they wear better than those of certain foreign pictures that are laid on thicker. In the art of animating his figures he approximates to the method of those two artists, at least in some of his more studied works; such as the Plague of Serpents at S. Bartolommeo, a picture full of horror. In every branch of the profession he has always the art to please; and it is astonishing that the man who led the way to a degenerate style at Venice, as Vasari is said to have done at Florence, and the Zuccàri at Rome, should still have retained so many of the attractions, both of nature and art, to delight the eye and affect the heart of the spectator. Guercino and Guido justly appreciated the powers of his pencil, when, on observing a picture of his at the Capuchins at Bologna, they exclaimed,—"What pity that such a master as this should ever have died!"*

* Among Palma's followers was Marco Boschino, who has furnished memoirs of certain artists of this third epoch, not to be met with in any other work. During this same epoch also flourished —Carlo Ridolfi, who wrote the "Lives of the Venetian Painters" —Pietro Vecchia—Gian Carlo Loth—Alessandro Veronese—Pietro Liberi—Alessandro Turchi—and Enea Salmeggia, styled il Talpino.

OF THE LOMBARD SCHOOLS.

On contemplating the principles and the progress of the art of painting in the Lombard states, I have arrived at this conclusion, that its history, as regards those states, ought to be handled in a way wholly different from that of other schools. The histories of the Florentine, Roman, Venetian, and Bolognese schools, may in some sort be looked upon as so many dramas, where the acts and the scenes are constantly shifting—such, in fact, being the different epochs into which each school is divided; and where fresh actors also are continually appearing upon the stage—for such are the masters comprised under each successive period; but the unity of place (the capital in each instance) is invariably preserved; and the principal actors, and, as it were, leading characters of the piece, always continue, if not to play a part, at least to hold out an example. With regard to the history of painting in Lombardy the case is otherwise; for Lombardy, which, in the infancy of the art, was split into many more independent states than it is at present, had in each of those states a school distinct from all the rest; and reckoned also distinct epochs; and if one of these schools may chance to have had some influence upon the style of another, this did not happen either so generally, or so immediately, as that many of them may be referred to the same epoch. Hence, I have been induced to renounce the common mode of expression—that of speaking of the Lombard school as if it were only one single school, and might be likened to that of Venice, for example, which, throughout the whole of the Venetian states, regarded as its greatest luminaries, first the Bellini, next Titian and his more distinguished contemporaries, then Palma; and which, moreover, adopted certain peculiarities in design, colouring, composition, and pencilling, by which it is easily distinguished from every other school. But in the Lombard school, as it is called, the case is different. Those founders of different schools, Leonardo, Giulio Romano, the Campi, Correggio, are too dissimilar to be referred to one common standard, or to one single epoch. I am aware that, as Correggio was a native of Lombardy, and the inventor of a new style which served as a model to great numbers in that part of Italy, the phrase Lombard school has been applied to those who adopted his maxims; and that the full contour, the jocund countenance, the rich and lucid colouring, the frequent foreshortenings, and, above all, the studied chiaroscuro, have been declared to be the characteristics of this school. But if we thus circumscribe the limits of the Lombard school, where shall we find room for the Mantuan artists, or for those of Milan and Cremona, and many more, who, having been born in Lombardy, and spent their lives there, as well as initiated numbers of their descendants in the art, are also entitled to a place among the Lombard painters?

For these reasons I have thought it best to treat of each school separately, and more or less diffusely, according as the number of artists it produced, and the details we have concerning them may seem to require.

MANTUAN SCHOOL.

EPOCH I.

MANTEGNA AND HIS SUCCESSORS.

I BEGIN with the Mantuan school, from which the two twin schools of Modena and Parma took their rise. As regards the art of painting, properly so called, I know of no artist who flourished at Mantua previous to Mantegna: all I can do, therefore, is to notice one or two anonymous works of the fourteenth and fifteenth centuries that have been preserved to our days. As regards the former of these two centuries, I saw in the cloister of S. Francesco a monument erected in 1303, above which was a Madonna surrounded by several Angels, figures of a rude and uncouth character, but exhibiting such strength and liveliness of colouring as could not fail to excite my surprise: nor have I any hesitation in referring to this monument as a proof that, in Lombardy, the restoration of painting had been effected by the unassisted efforts of its own inhabitants; inasmuch as this picture is of a date anterior to those of the Giotteschi scattered through Italy, and is also in a different style. In like manner, over an altar at S. Francesco, I saw another Madonna of the fifteenth century: whoever may have been its author, it proves that the art had already advanced beyond its infancy; although it had not yet reached that improved state to which it was carried by the celebrated Andrea Mantegna.

Mantegna.—Though the glory of having given birth to Mantegna can no longer be disputed with Padua, as was formerly the case, yet the seat of his school was Mantua, where, under the auspices of the Marquis Louis Gonzaga, he took up his abode with his family; though still without desisting from working at other places, especially at Rome. The works which he executed for Louis

cent VIII., in one of the chapels of the Vatican are still in being; and it is notorious, that in imitating the remains of antiquity, a point at which he constantly aimed, he acquired greater correctness in that city, owing to the multiplicity of ancient specimens with which it supplied him. He never deviated from the manner which I have already described on occasion of mentioning him at Padua as the scholar of Squarcione,* but went on continually improving upon it. There still exist at Mantua some of the works of his later years, and among these the picture of Victory, painted on canvass, is the most distinguished. The Virgin, accompanied by various Saints—among whom may be seen the Archangel Michael and St. Maurice in the act of supporting her robe—receives beneath it Francis Gonzaga, who is there represented in a kneeling posture, while she holds out her hand over him in token of taking him under her protection. Somewhat in the background may be observed St. Andrew and St. Longinus, the two patron saints of the city, and, before the throne, the infant St. John, together

* Lanzi's description of this style here alluded to is as follows:—"Mantegna tutto era in ricercare la castigatezza de' contorni, la beltà delle idee e de' corpi; ne solo adottava quella strettezza di vesti, quelle pieghe parallele, e quella diligenza di parti che degenera facilmente in secchezza; ma trascurava quella parte che anima le morte immagini, e cui diciamo espressione."

with S. Anna; at least, so Vasari and Ridolfi, who have not been over correct in their description of this picture, imagined; for the rosary which she holds in her hand makes us at once recognize in her the Princess-consort of the Marquis of Mantua, kneeling there with her husband. Mantua has not perhaps another painting so much visited and so much admired by foreigners as is this. Executed in 1495, it has sustained scarcely any injury during the three centuries that have elapsed since its completion. It is truly wonderful to observe the delicacy of the fleshes, the brightness of the armour, the diversified appearance of the drapery, and the dewy freshness of the fruits that have been introduced by way of ornament. Every head may serve as a model for vivacity and strength of character, and some of them even for the exact imitation they display of the antique: the design, both as regards the parts of the figure exposed to view and the drapery, exhibits in every part a softness and fulness which completely confutes the commonly received opinion, that the style of Mantegna and the dry style are one and the same thing. There is, moreover, a strength and richness of colouring, a delicacy of finish, and a gracefulness so peculiar, that to me it seems the last step in the art towards the perfection attained to by Da Vinci.

Nevertheless, his master-piece, according to

Vasari's opinion, was his Cæsar's Triumph, consisting of divers pieces, which, having been seized by the Germans during the sack of the city, in the end found their way into England. These works of Andrea's having perished, there still exist other considerable remains of his in one of the saloons of the castle, styled by Ridolfi the "Camera degli Sposi." We there meet with copious compositions in fresco; and among them portraits of certain of the Gonzaga family still in good preservation, together with a few Genii over one of the doors, in the last degree sprightly, airy, and jocund. In the different collections his works are more rarely to be met with than is usually imagined: genuine pictures of his may be recognized, not only by their elegance, the straightness of the folds of the drapery, or the yellowish cast of the landscape, sprinkled here and there with certain small and shapely pieces of rock; but also by the skilfulness of the design, and the delicacy of the pencilling. Nor do I think that he could have executed many cabinet pictures, taken up as he was with paintings on a larger scale, as well as with a multiplicity of engravings.

Andrea had no little influence upon the style of that age; and imitations of his manner are to be met with even beyond the limits of his school, which at Mantua was in very high repute. Francesco and another of his sons are reckoned among the best of his scholars. There is a writing of theirs extant, in which they engage to complete the works in the above-mentioned apartment at the castle, of which Andrea had painted only the walls. They there contributed the beautiful paintings on the ceiling. Whoever examines them must acknowledge that the art *del sotto in su*—the art of foreshortening objects on ceilings—of which the invention is usually ascribed to Melozio, was improved upon and almost brought to perfection by Mantegna and his sons.*

MANTUAN SCHOOL.

EPOCH II.

GIULIO ROMANO AND HIS FOLLOWERS.

The school of the *Mantegneschi* having become extinct at Mantua, another, more beautiful and more celebrated, started up in its stead,—one that might move the envy of Rome itself. Francis Gonzaga was succeeded in the dukedom by Fre-

* The other followers of Mantegna were—Carlo del Mantegna, Gianfrancesco and Giovanni Carotto, and Francesco and Girolamo Monsignori.

derick, a prince endowed with an elevation of mind and a passion for the fine arts, such that no artists of moderate talent could have carried his ideas into execution. By means of Baldassar Castiglione, previously an intimate friend of Raphael's, Giulio Romano was engaged to repair to Mantua, in the double character of engineer and painter to the Duke. The former of these employments occupied more of his time than the latter. The city, which had been damaged by the overflowing of the Mincio; the houses, which were insecure or ill-contrived; the style of architecture, which accorded but little with the dignity of a capital; continually supplied him with fresh matter on which to exercise his talents, and thus render himself in some sort a new founder of Mantua; insomuch that the Duke, in a transport of gratitude, was led to exclaim, that Giulio might more justly be called master of the city than he himself.

In the Roman school we treated of Giulio, as the scholar and heir of Raphael, as well as the person on whom devolved the completion of his works: here he is destined to figure as a master, who, both in his own performances and his instructions to others, pursues the method adopted by the great founder of his school. On his arrival in Mantua, he found there a rich store of the remains of antiquity, which afterwards went on continually increasing; and of which, the statues, busts, and bas-reliefs, now preserved in the academy, constitute but a small remnant. To these materials, collected by the Gonzaghi, he added a stock of his own. He was exceedingly rich in designs, copied not only from the remains of antiquity at Rome, but also from the works of Raphael. Nor did his own studies form a contemptible resource; there having been, as regards design, no one who succeeded better in combining fertility of fancy with choice, rapidity of execution with correctness, a thorough knowledge of mythology and history with a certain popular and familiar manner of handling them. After the death of his master he began to follow more freely the natural bent of his genius, which inclined him less to the graceful than the bold; leading him, in the execution of his works, to trust rather to the dexterity he had acquired by many years' practice, than to consult nature for their truth. To him, therefore, it was nothing more than mere play to bring the Ducal palace at Mantua, and the magnificent villa of the T,—to say nothing of his many other works,—to that high state of embellishment described by Vasari, and of which there still exist considerable remains. That multiplicity of chambers, with their gilded roofs; that infinity of beautiful stucco, from which so many casts have been taken for the instruction of beginners; that astonishing number of historical and fancy pieces, so well imagined and so well accommodated to each other; that endless variety of ornaments, adapted to so many situations and subjects,—all these form a complication of wonders, of which Giulio had the merit of being the sole author; for these vast works were all conceived, carried on, and completed by Giulio alone.

His practice was to prepare the cartoons himself, and then to give them to his scholars to execute, taking care afterwards to retouch the whole work with his own hand; thus correcting its defects, and impressing upon every part of it the stamp of his own elevated genius. It was Giulio's misfortune that his own touches at the palace of the T. were afterwards daubed over by the restorer's hand; whence the delightful fable of Psyche, the moral representations of human life, and that terrible Battle of the Giants with Jupiter, where he appears to defy Michael Angelo in robustness of manner, present us still with the composition and design, but not the pencilling, of Giulio. This we may better recognise at the Ducal palace, in his War of Troy, his story of Lucretia, and the little cabinets that he embellished with grotesques and the most ingenious fancy-pieces. There he might at one time be styled a Homer treating of warlike feats, at another, an Anacreon depicting scenes of debauchery and love. Nor was it a small portion of his time that he devoted to sacred subjects, especially for the cathedral, which, under the direction of the Duke's brother, Cardinal Gonzaga, he not only built, but also partly contributed to embellish; I say partly, for death prevented him from witnessing the completion of that admirable work. The pictures that he executed for other churches, with his own hand and without assistance, are not numerous: the three historical pieces on the subject of the Passion, painted in fresco at St. Mark's, are particularly pointed out as belonging to this class; as is also that St. Christopher over the large altar of the church of the same name, where he is represented as a man of great strength, and yet groaning under the weight of the Saviour of the world, whom he bears in the likeness of an infant upon his shoulders,—a legendary story originating in the name of Christopher. Giulio's followers at Mantua did not, as was the case elsewhere, mix up their master's method with those of other schools: on the contrary, they were most tenacious of their founder's style; insomuch, that in almost every head we may recognize the very same features as are most frequently found in his works; though their execution displays very different degrees of merit.

MODENESE SCHOOL.

EPOCH I.

THE OLD MASTERS.

The origin of this school might be deduced from the year 1235, if it were as certain that Berlinghieri reared up pupils in the state of Modena, as it is that in the town of Guiglia there is a St. Francis painted by him and bearing the date of the aforesaid year; but this may admit of a doubt. There is also another sacred piece referable to a Modenese painter,—a picture of the Virgin between two military Saints—which has been removed from Prague to the Imperial gallery at Vienna; on it is inscribed, in old characters, the two following lines:—

> Quis opus hoc finxit? Thomas de Mutina pinxit.
> Quale vides lector Barisini filius auctor.

After this picture of Tommaso's we must not omit to notice—a painting by Barnaba da Modena, preserved at Alba, bearing the name of the author and the date 1377; a work which has by one writer been preferred to those of Giotto,—and we cannot, as the case is, be Serafino de'

Serafini da Modena, containing various busts and full-lengths, and also bearing the name of the painter, and the date 1385. This latter is in the cathedral of Modena; and the principal subject is the Coronation of the Virgin. The composition is very similar to that observable in the works of Giotto and his school; to which indeed the general style of the picture approaches nearer than to that of any other school; save that the figures are stouter, and, if we may so say, better fed than those of the Florentines.*

. . . . . There was one advantage which Modena more especially enjoyed, even as early as the fifteenth century, and that was the possession of abundance of excellent modellers. In this art, which may be called the mother of sculpture and the nurse of painting, Modena has since produced the happiest specimens in the world; and this, if I mistake not, is the peculiar, the characteristic, and highest distinction of the school. Vasari has bestowed the warmest encomiums on Guido Mazzoni, otherwise styled Paganini, who as early as the year 1484 distinguished himself by a Holy Family at S. Margherita,—statues exhibiting an astonishing degree of vivacity and expression. The chronicler Lancillotto also awards high praise

* Lanzi here proceeds to recount the names of a number of artists down to the beginning of the sixteenth century, but none of them of any note.

to his contemporary Giovanni Abate, (the father of Niccolò Abate,) whose chalk models of sacred subjects were held in the greatest esteem; especially his Crucifixions, where every vein and every nerve was given with the most scrupulous regard to anatomy. He, however, was far surpassed by Antonio Begarelli, probably his scholar, who, by means of his models, consisting of figures as large as life, and even larger, has almost borne away the palm from every other competitor. The Benedictine Fathers possess a great many of them both in their church and monastery. He lived to a great age, and filled the churches of Modena with monuments, crucifixes, groups, and isolated statues; to say nothing of what he executed at Parma, Mantua, and other places. Vasari eulogizes him for the "fine air of his heads, the beauty of his draperies, the exquisite proportion of his figures, and the exactness with which he imitated the colour of marble;" relating that even Buonarroti "looked upon these works as possessing great merit," and exclaimed:—"Could this clay but be converted into marble, then woe to the statues of antiquity!" I know not what higher encomium can be produced in favour of any artist; especially when I reflect how profound a connoisseur Buonarroti was, and how little prodigal of praise. Finally, we ought to add, that Begarelli was eminently skilled in design, and that he instructed the rising generation in that branch of art as well as in modelling. Hence he had great influence on the art of painting; and to him, in great measure, is attributed the correctness, the relief, the skilful foreshortening, and the gracefulness, (bordering almost on Raphael's,) for which this part of Lombardy is distinguished.

MODENESE SCHOOL.

EPOCH II.

DURING THE SIXTEENTH CENTURY, RAPHAEL AND CORREGGIO ARE THE MODELS LOOKED UP TO BY THIS SCHOOL.

No city of Lombardy became familiar with Raphael's style earlier than Modena, nor did any city of Italy become more deeply enamoured of that style, or produce successful imitators of it in greater number.

Pellegrino da Modena, denominated, in Lancellotti's chronicle, degli Aretusi, otherwise de' Munari, had acquired the rudiments of art in his native place, and, as early as the year 1509, had executed there the picture that is now to be seen in S. Giovanni's, and in the highest state of preservation—a sufficient evidence of the great attainments of its author even previous to his entering

Raphael's school. Such, however, was the progress he made in that school, that his master availed himself of his assistance even in the *Loggie* of the Vatican itself; while he also carried on other works at Rome, at one time in conjunction with Perino del Vaga, at another without any assistance. In some of those works of his at S. Giacomo degli Spagnuoli, there were figures exhibiting the utmost gracefulness of manner, and almost bordering on Raphael's style, according to Titi's account, who deplores the injudicious restoration of them. His merit, however, cannot so well be judged of at Rome as at his native place; especially in the church of S. Paolo, where there is a Nativity that breathes throughout the grace of Raphael. This unfortunate man had a son, whom, in consequence of a murder he had committed, the relatives of the deceased eagerly sought after, with intent to lay violent hands on him; but falling in with the father, they wreaked their vengeance upon him, and put him to death: this tragical event occurred in the year 1523. Pellegrino's instructions were of no small benefit to Giulio Taraschi, some of whose pictures still exist in St. Peter's at Modena, executed in the style of the Roman school; a style which he is said to have transmitted to two brothers of his, as well as to others.

Somewhat subsequent to this, Correggio began

to be looked up to as a model in the Modenese school, where he was person for its brightest ornament. This master painted a great many works at Parma, and under the head of the Parmesan school we shall have to take especial notice of him; but he also wrought at Modena, Reggio, Carpi, and Correggio. Thus he began betimes to produce a visible influence on the Modenese school, and to be looked up to there as a master whose manner might be followed with advantage, either by emulating it in all its parts, or by combining it with that of Raphael.

This was more especially the case when, Correggio being now no more, his reputation began to increase; and when all the best works that he had left in the capital and the neighbouring cities were gradually brought together by the Dukes of the house of Este and deposited in their gallery, where they remained till near the middle of the present (eighteenth) century.* At that time Modena was frequented by painters of every nation, who went thither to copy those divine originals, and observe the art with which they were executed; nor did the Modenese themselves neglect to profit by them; vestiges of Correggio's style being discoverable in the works of almost every one of those

* Francis III. sold to the court of Dresden a hundred pictures—among which were five Correggios—for a hundred-and-thirty thousand Venetian sequins.

artists. Nevertheless, when speaking of the other masters, we must acknowledge them to evince a more decided bent and predilection for Raphael and the Roman style; whether it be that we usually set a higher value upon the merits of strangers, than upon those of our own countrymen; or that none but Pellegrino's followers continued for any great length of time to afford instruction to the rising generation, and to maintain their credit in those parts.

NICCOLÒ DELL' ABATE.

Let us now turn to Niccolò dell' Abate, whom we must notice somewhat more fully, as befits the dignity of a painter esteemed by Algarotti as "one of the greatest masters the world has ever seen." Some have imagined that he received the rudiments of art from Correggio, a point which cannot altogether be denied, more firmly on account of certain of his foreshortenings and the bold relief of his pictures. Vasari, however, says not a word of his having derived instruction from that source; merely observing, on occasion of mentioning the Martyrdom of St. Peter and St. Paul painted by him for the Black Friars, that the figure of one of the executioners is taken from a picture of Correggio's placed in the church of S. Giovanni at Parma. But whoever may have been Niccolino's master, in his frescos at Modena, which are reckoned among his earliest performances, he discovers an evident predilection for the Roman school. The same observation applies to those twelve frescos of his from the twelve books of the Æneid, which, having been severed from the wall on which they were painted in the fortress of Scandiano, now adorn the Ducal gallery; and might alone suffice to establish his reputation for figures, landscapes, architectural ornaments, animals, every attainment, in short, meet for an accomplished follower of Raphael. On arriving at man's estate, having proceeded to Bologna, where he took up his abode, he painted, under the portico de' Leoni, a Nativity, in a style such that, neither in those of Raffaellino del Borgo, nor those of any other artist, though educated at Rome, have I been able to discover so strong a resemblance to Raphael's manner as in this. I am aware, too, that a distinguished artist used to call it the best fresco in all Bologna. It was the delight and the model of the Caracci, no less than the other works that Niccolino left in that city. Among those the most admired by foreigners is that Conversazione which serves as a frieze to the Sala of the Institute. Next to Raphael, this artist did not refuse to imitate others also. There is a well-known sonnet* of Agostino Carracci's, which many a painter has got by heart, where the author professes to have found combined in Niccolino alone the symmetry of Raphael, the terrible of M. Angelo, Titian's truth, Coreggio's elevation, the composition of Tibaldi, and the grace of Parmigianino: in a word, the best of every artist and of every school. The opinion here expressed,—though the lines must be taken as the effusion of a poet, and that poet a passionate admirer of one who did honour to his school—would find more supporters, were Niccolino's works more frequently to be found in the different collections. They are, however, very rarely to be met with, both because he almost al-

* Chi farsi un buon pittor brama e desia,
Il disegno di Roma abbia alla mano;
La mossa coll' ombrar Veneziano,
E il degno colorir di Lombardia;
Di Michelangiol la terribil via,
Il vero natural di Tiziano,
Di Coreggio lo stil puro e sovrano,
E di un Raffael la vera simmetria;
Del Tibaldi il decoro e il fondamento,
Del dotto Primaticcio l'inventare,
E un po' di grazia del Parmigianino:
Ma senza tanti studi e tanto stento,
Si ponga solo l'opre ad imitare
Che qui lasciocci il nostro Niccolino.

ways wrought in fresco, and because at the age of forty he passed over into France. Thither he had been invited by the Abate Primaticcio to assist him in the great works he was then executing for Charles IX., nor did he ever set eyes on Italy again. Hence arose the story that he was Primaticcio's scholar, and that he was therefore called l'Abate; whereas he derived that epithet from his own family. The historical pieces, eight-and-thirty in number, relative to Ulysses, painted by Niccolò from Primaticcio's designs, and forming the most extensive of all the many works he executed in France, were still in being at Fontainebleau about the year 1740; these works, according to Algarotti, were subsequently defaced, but they may still be seen in the engravings taken from them by Van Tulden, the scholar of Rubens.

Lelio Orsi.—Shortly afterwards Lelio Orsi of Reggio began to come into repute; being banished from his native-place, he repaired to Novellara,—a town at that time under the sway of the Gonzaghi,—and there took up his abode; whence he is commonly styled Lelio da Novellara. Whether this distinguished painter were a disciple of Correggio's or not, is a matter of doubt; some biographers affirming it, others denying it. From the time and place at which he lived, he may well have been acquainted with him; moreover he studied, and took designs from his works; and there is still in the possession of the noble family of Gazzola at Parma, a copy by him of Correggio's celebrated Night. Nor are there wanting those who affirm that Lelio left specimens of his art at Parma, where the brightest ornaments of the school have employed their pencil. Various apocryphal tales have been, and still are, current concerning him; as, that he was the scholar of M. Angelo; that Correggio used to correspond with him, and even consult him on the subject of design. True, indeed, it is, that his design is of an ingenious, studied, and bold character; whether this arose from his having been at Rome, as Tiraboschi, on the faith of a certain manuscript, contended; or that he acquired this style from Giulio Romano at Mantua; or that he had seen M. Angelo's models and designs,—great minds requiring nothing more than a knowledge of the right path, to enable them to pursue it with success. His design is evidently not in the Lombard style; and hence arises the great difficulty in the way of our supposing him to be a scholar of Correggio's; for had such been the case, his earlier works at least would not have displayed so bold a character. Nevertheless, some have supposed him to imitate Correggio, whether in grandeur of chiaroscuro, the thick-laying on of his colours, or the beauty and charms of some of his youthful heads. Reggio, and more especially Novellara, possessed a good many frescos of his, which have now in great part perished. But few of his altar-pieces remain in public in these two cities; the rest having been removed. Others that pass for his at Parma, Ancona, and Mantua, are by no means well authenticated; and there is every reason to suppose that Lelio, having spent his days at Reggio and Novellara, never removed from them either very far or for any great length of time; and thus continued to be less known than many painters of a lower grade.

MODENESE SCHOOL.

EPOCH III.

THE MODENESE PAINTERS OF THE SEVENTEENTH CENTURY FOLLOW FOR THE MOST PART THOSE OF BOLOGNA.

During the seventeenth century, Modena and its dependencies had not wholly abandoned the style introduced by Munari, or that introduced by Correggio and Lelio; having still had to boast of some disciples and followers of these masters: these styles, however, became less prevalent in proportion as the *Carracceschi* began to gain ground and to influence by their example the other schools of Italy. We know that some of the Modenese painters frequented their schools; and Bartolomeo Schedone is by Malvasia reckoned among the disciples of the Caracci.

SCHEDONE.

Supposing Malvasia to be correct in thus referring Schedone to the school of the Caracci, we must either come to the conclusion that his earlier performances are unknown, or that he had scarcely crossed the threshold of that school; whereas, even in those larger works that are pointed out as his, it is rare that we can discover any vestiges of the style of the Caracci. It would rather appear that he took for his models those of his countrymen who imitated Raphael, but that the model that he looked up to most of all was Correggio, of whose originals there were so many to be found at Modena. His frescos executed at the Palazzo Pubblico in competition with Ercole Abati about the year 1604, are still in being; among them is the beautiful story of Coriolanus, and the Seven Women, intended as a personification of Concord; whoever takes the trouble to examine them, will find them to combine the two characters abovementioned. There is, moreover, at the cathedral, a half-length figure of S. Geminiano with an Infant that he has just restored to life, who is taking hold of his crook, and, as it were, expressing his gratitude: it is one of his happiest performances, and might almost pass for a work of Coreggio's. This successful imitation of Coreggio's style, afforded matter of commendation even at that time in other pictures of his despatched to different places; and Marini speaks of it in one of his letters as altogether wonderful. Scannelli, who wrote about forty years after the death of Schedone, joins in this panegyric; though, to render the imitation complete, he could have wished it had been founded more on experience and principle; where I suspect he refers to the design and the perspective, in which Schedone sometimes falls into error. For the rest, his figures display much gracefulness of character and of action; and his colouring, as regards his frescos, is of the gayest and most lively kind; in his oil paintings it is of a more sober cast, though more perfectly blended, and not always exempt from those faults occasioned by the defective nature of the grounds employed in the age of the Carracci. His larger pictures, such as the Pietà now in the Academy of Parma, are exceedingly scarce: his historical pieces such as, at Loreto, the Nativity of Christ and that of the

Virgin, placed as accompaniments to a painting of Filippo Bellini, are also very rarely to be seen. Holy Families of his, and similar small pictures on sacred subjects, are now and then to be met with, but not in any great number, and are very highly prized; insomuch that, according to Tiraboschi, for one of them was asked no less a sum than four thousand crowns. The collection of the King of Naples possesses several of them, that collection having been enriched, not only with the other pictures belonging to the Farnese family, but with those also which Schedone, while in the service of the Duke Ranuccio, the most liberal of his patrons, had painted for that family. This artist neither lived to any great age nor produced any great number of works, being diverted from his studies by the love of play; owing to his passion for which, having lost a large sum of money, he died of grief towards the close of the year 1615.*

* The other most distinguished artists of this epoch, were Camillo Gavassetti, Lodovico Lana and Giacomo Cavedone.

PARMESAN SCHOOL.

EPOCH I.

THE OLD MASTERS.

Next after the school of Modena I place that of Parma, and the neighbouring territory; and willingly would I join them together as others have done, if, together with difference of government, I did not also find a difference of manner; it being my opinion, as I have already stated, that Raphael's style predominated in the former, Correggio's in the latter. Correggio is the founder of the Parmesan school, where, for several generations, he has had a succession of followers so addicted to his manner, that they would seem to have looked to no one else. In what condition he found the art on his arrival at Parma, may be inferred from those old pictures scattered through the city, which assuredly do not display a degree of progress equal to that of some other of the Italian schools. Not that Parma was not quickly alive to the art of design. As early as the twelfth century there flourished there one Benedetto Antelami, of whom there still remains in the cathedral a bas-relief representing the Crucifixion of our

Sacrum; it is the production of a rude age; but from that period down to the time of Giovanni Pisano, I doubt whether I have ever met with any piece of sculpture to equal it. With regard to painting itself, the illustrious P. Affò has brought to light particulars of the most interesting character, from published and unpublished records, in order to prove that both single figures and historical pieces were executed at Parma previous to the year 1233. On the completion of the baptistery in 1260, that collection of paintings was executed there, which, as far as regards the old style, may now-a-days be looked upon as one of the finest monuments to be met with in Upper Italy. The subjects are such as were most in vogue at the time; the style is less angular and rectilinear than that of the Greek workers in mosaic; and evinces some degree of originality in the drapery, the decoration, and the composition: above all, it displays a rare degree of skill in the mechanical execution of the gilding and the colouring; which, in spite of the lapse of five centuries, is still in very tolerable preservation.

On coming down to more recent times, we find, in many places, both at Placentia and Parma, no lack of pictures executed by painters of the thirteenth century, sometimes with dates on which we can rely, sometimes without. Those of Placentia are in the church and convent of the *Benedictines*;

but the best preserved is an altar-piece at St. Antony's the Martyr, with historical pieces relative to that Saint, in figures of a diminutive size, very tolerably executed, and with drapery of such a character, that in these figures we behold the usages, which were, if we may so say, municipal and peculiar to the place. Parma possesses some of the same age; and certain others still in being at the church of St. Francis, in a somewhat more refined style, must be referred to Bartolommeo Grossi, or Jacopo Loschi, his son-in-law, who painted there in 1462.*

PARMESAN SCHOOL.

EPOCH II.

ANTONIO ALLEGRI,

COMMONLY CALLED CORREGGIO.

We come now to an artist, whom, in consideration of his great celebrity and the influence his works had, and still have, over the style of painting in Italy, it is impossible to dismiss with our usual brevity.

* Lanzi here records a few others of the earlier artists of this school, but none of any note; among them are Marmitta, the supposed master of Parmigianino.

Scannelli, Orlandi, and others, have censured Vasari for exaggerating the lowliness of Antonio's station in life, who, in fact, was born in an illustrious city of a very respectable family, and not wholly destitute of fortune; whence he received in his boyhood an education sufficient to account for his future progress. They have also reproached him with excessive credulity, for describing Correggio as of a miserly and melancholy temperament, and groaning, as it were, under the weight of a large family; for describing him, too, as having been very little in request, and badly paid; whereas, say they, we know that he was in favour with the great, and rewarded with considerable sums for his works; insomuch that he was enabled to leave a handsome fortune to his family. Now, though I recognize something of exaggeration in Vasari's statements, yet I cannot think them altogether unfounded: and whoever will take the trouble to compare the orders and the gains of Correggio with those of Raphael, Michael Angelo, Titian, and even Vasari himself, will no longer wonder that that biographer should have shown signs of commiserating his hard fortune. The largest payments made to Correggio have been ascertained. For the cupola and the larger nave of the church of S. Giovanni, he received four hundred and seventy-two gold ducats, or Roman sechins; and for the cupola of the cathedral, three hundred and fifty—considerable sums certainly; but as he was occupied from the year 1520 to 1530, on the sketches and execution of these great works, he could undertake but few others, and those not of a very lucrative kind. His celebrated *Night* brought him forty gold ducats; his St. Jerome, on which he spent six months, brought him, besides his subsistence for those six months, forty-seven ducats or zechins; and after the same proportion we may calculate the time he spent upon his other smaller works, and the prices he received for them. Something more he may have received for the two pictures he painted for the Duke of Modena, but these were the only works he ever executed for a sovereign prince. All this being considered, it seems incredible that, after deducting what he must have spent upon colours, models, assistants, and the maintenance of his family, he could still have had so much left, as to be able to leave that family in a state of affluence.

For my part, even though I were to admit the truth of all that has been said of the poverty of this great man, so far from thinking it a disgrace to him, I should think it did him honour, when I reflect that, notwithstanding all this penury, he painted with a prodigality of manner of which there is no other example. Every picture of his is executed either on copper, panel, or canvass, of the finest kind, with a profusion of ultramarine, foreshortening, and the most beautiful graces; with a full well-fed pencil, and the utmost carefulness of finishing; and, for the most part, without his having ever desisted from the work till he had fully completed it: in a word, without any of that stint, either of expense or time, with which almost every other artist is chargeable. Generosity like this might do honour to a wealthy individual who painted merely for his own amusement; how much more commendable then is it in one whose means were so limited! To my mind, it shows a degree of magnanimity worthy of a genuine Spartan.

There is a tradition at Correggio, that Antonio received the first rudiments of art from his uncle Lorenzo; after which, if we may depend upon the account transmitted by Vedriani, he went to Modena, where he frequented the school of Francesco Bianchi, called Il Frari, who died in 1510. It would seem, too, that he there made himself acquainted with the plastic art, which at that time happened to be in high repute there; whence, in conjunction with Begarelli, he afterwards executed the group of the Pietà at S. Margherita, of which the three most beautiful figures are ascribed to Correggio. In the same seat of learning, too, I suspect it was that he laid the foundation of those accomplishments discoverable in his works, where we may trace a competent knowledge of geometry in his perspectives, of architecture in his edifices, and of poetry in his gay and charming imagery. After this, his biographers, judging from certain works in his earlier style, will have it that he went to Mantua to the academy of Andrea Mantegna; but the recent discovery that Andrea died in 1506, overthrows this supposition. To me, however, it appears highly probable that he derived that first manner from the works Mantegna left at Mantua, and in support of this opinion I here adduce a few arguments. The most remarkable of all Mantegna's performances was his picture of Victory; of this various imitations are to be found in the works of Coreggio, the most palpable of which may be observed in the S. Giorgio of Dresden. That exquisite taste which Coreggio invariably displays in his canvass, in the thick laying on of his colours, and the high finish of his pictures, excites our astonishment, and seems inexplicable: there is, however, no longer any thing mysterious in the matter, if we suppose him to have taken Andrea for his model, who surpassed every other artist in these particulars. Let us, moreover, take into account the grace and hilarity which Coreggio imparted to his compositions, investing them with a sort of rainbow-like colouring, characterizing them by a certain studied introduction of every species of foreshortening, embellishing them with infantine figures remarkable for their vivacity, as well as with fruits and other pleasing objects; and I should then like to know whether this new style of his may not be considered as truly an improvement and a perfecting of Mantegna's style, as Raphael's and Titian's pictures may of those of Perugino and Gio. Bellini.

As to his having received instruction from Mantegna himself, the prevailing opinion in Lombardy now is, that Vedriani was mistaken, having been led into error by the name; and that he called Andrea the master of Correggio, whereas he ought to have said it was Francesco his son, with whom it is recorded Allegri resided some time, either as a pupil or an assistant. This school had made great advances, and had even forestalled Melozio, and produced some tolerable specimens in that species of foreshortening called *di sotto in su*; there now remained but one step more to take in order to arrive at the modern style; and this step a man of Correggio's genius would naturally make, just as the other great painters of that age did in the rest of the Italian schools. In fact, even in his very first essays, he seems to have aimed at a softer and fuller style than Mantegna's; and some, among whom is the Abate Bettinelli, have pointed out a few examples of this in Mantua. In that town I also saw, in the possession of the Abate Bettinelli, a small picture of a Holy Family, which was about to be engraved; and in which, with the exception of some little stiffness in the drapery, every part tends to the modern manner. The Ducal gallery at Modena contains another Madonna or two of Coreggio's, which may be referred to this period; while other works of his are pointed out in various places: among these there was at Milan, where it was seen and recognized for genuine by the Abate Carlo Bianconi, a small picture representing our Saviour taking leave of the Virgin Mother previous to his crucifixion. There must no doubt be many pictures of Coreggio's of inferior rank, and those scattered about here and there, and either such as are still unknown, or whose authenticity is disputed; Vasari having recorded of him that he produced a great many different works (molte pitture e opere).

How comes it, then, that in the published catalogues we find so small a number of pictures attributed to him, and those almost all of first-rate merit? Doubtless, because all that are not superlatively good are deemed unworthy of so celebrated a man, and are either confidently denied to be his, or considered to be of questionable authenticity, or else are ascribed to his scholars. Mengs himself, who made such diligent inquiries after the remains of this artist, and yet showed so much caution in admitting any of his controverted works, knew of but one picture in his first style, and that was the St. Anthony of the Dresden gallery, which, together with the St. Francis and the Virgio, he painted at Carpi in the year 1512, when only eighteen years of age. From the dryness he remarked in this, and the richness and mellowness (morbidezza) he generally found in his other paintings, Mengs conjectured that Correggio's transition from his first to his second style, must have been a sudden one; and set himself to discover the mysterious cause. He supposed, therefore, that there was some truth in that which, in opposition to the authority of Vasari, had been first asserted by De Piles in his Dissertations, as well as by Resta and one or two others,—that Correggio had visited Rome; and that, having there attentively observed the remains of antiquity, as well as the works of Raphael and Michael Angelo, and the foreshortenings of Melozzo, he returned to Lombardy with a taste wholly different from that which he had carried with him to Rome.

That distinguished individual, however, did not hazard this conjecture without considerable hesitation; and not only permitted his reader to hold the contrary hypothesis, but even hinted at one of the arguments by which it might be defended; for thus he expresses himself:—"If he did not see the remains of antiquity such as they exist at Rome, he at least saw them as they exist at Modena or Parma: to a man of genius the mere indication of improvement in any given object is sufficient to give him an idea of what that object may be brought to." It will not be difficult to bring forward examples to corroborate this assertion. Titian and Tintoretto, by the help of casts, surpassed others who designed statues; Baroccio, having chanced to obtain a transient view of one of Coreggio's heads, became eminent in the very same style. And, if we may borrow from the sciences another example of the capabilities of transcendant genius, Galileo, by observing the oscillation of a lamp in one of the Pisan churches, deduced from it the theory of motion and the principles of the new philosophy. In the same manner, from certain faint indications of it, might the idea of a new style have been conceived by this consummate artist, who, even in Vasari's time, "was looked up to as something superhuman." Nor indeed was it a slight impulse, but a sufficiently powerful one, that he may well be supposed to have received from the fine works of Mantegna; from the remains of ancient art collected in Mantua and Parma; from the studios of the Mantegni and Begarelli, rich both in casts and designs; from intercourse with artists who had been at Rome, with Munari and Giulio himself; and, lastly, from the prevailing feeling of the age, which, dissatisfied with the meagreness of the older method, every where aimed at greater fulness, softness, and clearness of contour. By these various helps the improvement that still remained to be

much was rendered sufficiently easy to a Correggio; but in a still greater degree was it facilitated by his transcendent genius. This led him to contemplate nature with the same eye that the ancient Greeks and the great Italians of modern times had contemplated it. The greatest men have sometimes, even without any communication with each other, trod in the same steps, or, as Cicero expresses it, "Quadam ingenii divinitate in eadem vestigia inciderunt." But of this no more at present, as we shall have to treat of it afresh a few pages hence. Here it remains for us to examine whether Correggio's transition from the old to the new style was a sudden one, or whether it was a work of time.

I could have wished that Mengs had seen certain fresco paintings said to have been executed by Antonio in his earlier days for the Marchesa Gambara, a Correggese lady, and which have since perished: these would doubtless have enabled him to throw some light on the subject. I could have wished, at any rate, that he had fallen in with two pictures executed by Antonio in his native place, and discovered within these few years: in these he would probably have detected that middle path which subsists between the St. Anthony and the St. George of Dresden. The genuineness of the first is called in question by Tiraboschi; there being an authentic document to assign it to

Correggio. For my part, I think we should admit it to be genuine until either weighty reasons, or the authority of practical professors, can be produced to the contrary. It was formerly in the oratory of the Misericordia, and old copies of it are still preserved in several houses at Correggio. It consists of a very beautiful landscape with four Saints, St. Peter, St. Margaret, the Magdalen, and another, whom I take to be St. Raymond, though not contemporary with the Apostles. The St. Peter bears some resemblance to that of Mantegna's, in his Ascension at St. Andrea's; while in the thicket also, and in the nature of the ground, we discover a remarkable conformity with Mantegna's manner. This picture having been blackened by the smoke of the tapers continually burning before it, or, as some suspect, by a varnish laid on for the express purpose of concealing its value and preventing it from being taken away, it was found necessary to remove it from the altar as useless, and in its stead to substitute a copy, in which the last figure is changed into a St. Ursula. The original subsequently fell into the hands of Sig. Antonio Armanno, one of the profoundest connoisseurs in engravings of the present day; and not less skilful in appreciating the works of ancient painters than in the art of cleaning them. After the persevering labour of a year, he succeeded in removing from the picture the veil that concealed it; and so beautiful has it now become once more, that crowds of accomplished foreigners are continually flocking to admire it. It is said to exhibit greater softness (morbidezza) than the St. Anthony of the Dresden gallery; though it is still very inferior to the St. Giorgio and others of the same stamp.

About the same time Allegri painted at Correggio, for the church of the Conventuals, an ancona, or sort of little wooden altar, consisting of three pictures. It seems certain, that the two pictures above-mentioned opened the way to this employment; for, from the written agreement it appears, that he was then twenty years of age; and yet, such was the high opinion entertained of his merits, that the stipulated price was a hundred gold ducats; in other words, a hundred sequins. He there depicted St. Bartholomew and St. John, one on each side; while in the middle piece he represented a Repose of the Holy Family during the Flight into Egypt, adding to this last a figure of St. Francis. Francis I., Duke of Modena, was greatly taken with this picture; and, sending Boulanger thither under pretext of making a copy of it, he contrived to possess himself of the original; dexterously substituting the copy itself in its place,—a wrong which he afterwards repaired by a grant to the convent of certain lands. It is supposed that the picture was afterwards sent to the

Modenese family, and that the house of Este received from that family, in exchange, Andrea del Sarto's Sacrifice of Abraham. The fact is, that it was in the Royal gallery of Florence as early as the seventeenth century; and Barri, who saw it there, speaks of it with commendation in his pictorial tour as an original. In process of time, however, because it happened to be less perfect than the most perfect of Correggio's works, it was less highly prized; nay, even its author's name was changed, and by some it was pointed out as a Baroccio, by others as a Vanni. Sig. Armanno, whom we have just noticed, who happened to recollect the copy then retained at Correggio, discovered this hidden treasure. At first its authenticity was disputed, chiefly on the ground that Allegri had painted it on panel, whereas the Medicean picture was on canvas. This objection, however, fell to the ground on comparing it with Boulanger's copy, which is also on canvas; for, most naturally, had the original been on wood, the copyist could not have succeeded in palming upon the monks, in whose church it was placed, a canvas painting in its stead. The probability of its genuineness becomes greater when we reflect, that no other gallery ever produced a similar Repose, to dispute the originality with that of Florence, as has happened, and still happens, in the case of certain pictures repeated in different places.

Indeed, we have sufficient proofs of its originality, in the traces it exhibits of Correggio's pencilling, in the remains of a varnish peculiar to that artist, and in the general style of colouring as compared with his works at Parma. All, however, are agreed that this work may be considered as holding a middle place between his first and second styles; and whoever compares it with that other Repose in the church of S. Sepolcro at Parma, commonly called the Madonna della Scodella, will find considerable difference between them; just as he will find considerable difference between Raphael's paintings at Città di Castello and his paintings at Rome.

Mengs notices two other pictures that may be included in the same class; the one is the Noli me tangere, which was removed from the Casa Ercolani to the Escurial; the other is a picture of the Virgin in the act of adoring the Infant Saviour, and is in the Royal gallery at Florence; both of them in a taste which he looked for in vain in Correggio's more sublime and celebrated works. To these we may add the Martyrs in the possession of the Litta family at Milan, and certain others of Correggio's pictures noticed in Tiraboschi's catalogue, which is the fullest of any extant. In short, it seems that we must admit, even in this painter, a middle style between the one which he adopted as a scholar, and the one which he carried to perfection as a master. I cannot but think there is much truth in a remark I once heard made—that Correggio essayed a variety of styles before he fixed upon that which characterises him; and that this is the reason why he appears, to some, to be not merely one but several painters. He was possessed with an idea of the beautiful and the perfect, partly derived from other artists, partly the work of his own imagination; an idea which cannot possibly be executed without much time and labour; whence he was constrained to imitate the natural philosopher, who makes a hundred different experiments, and tries a hundred different schemes, before he hits upon the object he has in view.

In a transition thus gradual, and in an artist who in each succeeding effort surpassed his previous performances, it is no easy task to fix the precise epoch of his new style. I once saw at Rome a very beautiful little picture, representing in the back-ground, the Praying of Christ in the Garden, and in the foreground, the Youth who in his flight leaves his mantle behind him; a work, the original of which is in England, while at Milan may be seen a duplicate in the possession of Count Kevenuller. The one at Rome bore, in old characters, the date of 1505, a date unquestionably false. The date inscribed on the Nuptials of St. Catherine, in the possession of Count

Brühl, formerly first minister to the king of Poland—a picture exactly corresponding with the one at Capo di Monte,—bears a greater appearance of truth: this date gives the year 1517. In that year, which was the twenty-third of the painter's age, it is not unlikely that he had pretty well matured his new style; since about the year 1518 or 1519, he executed at Parma the picture which still remains in the monastery of S. Paolo. This picture, after many disputes, has recently been recognized as "one of the most spirited, one of the noblest and most erudite performances that ever proceeded from the hand of its incomparable author;" it has moreover been illustrated, and its true date ascertained, in an excellent little work by the Padre Affò. This work is of some import to our history. There it is explained how Correggio might very well have imitated the ancients merely by the use of such helps as he met with at Parma; as well as how we may account for the serious difficulty arising from the silence of Mengs, who saw this picture without enumerating it among the rest of Antonio's works. There, too, we find explained that other difficulty, namely, how a Chase of Diana, with that multitude of Cupids accompanying the goddess, and those other profanities distributed over various lunettes in the same chamber—the Graces, the Fates, the Vestals in the act of sacrificing, Juno suspended from heaven in a state of nudity, exactly as described in the fifteenth book of Homer's Iliad, and other subjects of the like nature, not at all becoming a religious establishment—could ever have been painted for a convent. Our wonder ceases on learning that this convent was the residence of an abbess, in an age when the nuns of St. Paul's were under very little restraint ([illegible]); when every abbess was elected for life, had jurisdiction over lands and villages, and lived almost as a secular personage.

This undertaking, so admirably executed by Correggio at St. Paul's, served to recommend him to the Padri Cassinensi, who made choice of him for the great work at the church of St. John; a work determined upon in the year 1520, and finished in 1524; as is evident from the archives. There, in addition to several minor works, he decorated the tribune; which was afterwards taken down for the purpose of lengthening the choir, and replaced by another, the decorations of which were by Aretusi. On the demolition of the tribune, the Coronation of the Virgin, which formed the most important part of this decoration, was saved, and may still be seen in the Royal library; several heads of angels also, which in like manner escaped the wreck, are preserved in the Rondanini palace at Rome. Of Correggio's performances in the church of St. John, there still exist, in one of the chapels, two pictures placed opposite to each other—a Descent from the Cross and the Martyrdom of S. Placido—painted on canvas made for the purpose, as was the case with some of Mantegna's pictures. Outside another chapel, is a St. John the Evangelist, a figure in the sublimest style. Lastly, there is the great cupola, on which he represented Christ Ascending to the Father, and the Apostles looking up with mingled feelings of veneration and astonishment; and this work whether we consider the proportions and foreshortening of the figures, the anatomy, the drapery, or the whole together, was, in its kind, a miracle of art without example; for Michael Angelo's terrible *Last Judgment* in the Vatican was not yet in being.

Yet admirable as was this work, it was forced to yield the palm to another of Correggio's, (for none but he could have surpassed it,) and that was the Assumption of the Virgin, in the cathedral of Parma, finished in 1530. This work is on a much larger scale than the preceding; and here, too, according to the usual custom, in the lower part of the picture the same Apostles are introduced, in attitudes of wonder and adoration; yet in such a manner as to make them totally distinct from the former. In the upper part of the picture he portrayed an immense multitude of Blessed Spirits grouped and disposed in the happiest man-

ies, together with a crowd of Angels and Cherubs, all of them in action; some sustaining the Virgin and aiding her flight, others dancing and making melody, others again celebrating the glorious spectacle with shouts and songs of praise. Over these heads there is diffused a loveliness, an air of joy and festivity, and over the whole picture such a radiant light, that though it has suffered greatly, it still acts like magic upon the spectator, and makes him almost fancy himself in heaven. These great works, as is reported also of those in the Chambers of Raphael, contributed not a little to the elevation of his style; and, in the difficult art of fresco painting, carried him to the highest pitch of perfection. It is well worth while to examine them near at hand, and mark the boldness and confidence of the pencilling: to observe also those parts that at a distance appear so beautiful, indicated by a few slight touches; and see that beautiful colouring, as well as that harmony which unites so many objects in one, produced, as it were, in mere sport. Correggio survived four years after he had finished the cupola of the cathedral; nor did he, during all this time, ever commence the painting of the tribune, which he had undertaken to do, and for which indeed he had received a part of the pay, though this was afterwards refunded by his heirs. It is conjectured that those who conducted the works caused him some disgust; for we find Soiaro, on being invited to paint at the Steccata, making difficulties and taking certain precautions, not choosing "to be subjected to the caprice of so many different heads; and you know (continues he in a letter to one of his friends) what was said to Correggio in the cathedral." This must have been some insulting observation that disheartened and disgusted him; probably that which one of the workmen, who disapproved of the smallness of his figures, is said to have cast in his teeth:—*Ci avete fatto un guazzetto di rane*,—"Why, you have given us here a hash of frogs"—a senseless sneer, for which Correggio might easily have consoled himself. One workman did not constitute the whole of Parma.

He died, however, four years afterwards, in his native place, at the age of forty-four, without having completed the work, and without having left us any portrait of himself that can be considered as genuine.

Mengs, who analysed the last and most perfect of Correggio's styles, as he did also in the case of Titian and Raphael, assigns him, in this triumvirate of painters, the next place after Raphael; observing, that the latter depicted more exquisitely than he the effects of moral feeling, though in the expression of corporeal feeling he was inferior to him. In this branch of art Correggio was inimitable; contriving by means of his colouring, and yet more by means of his chiaroscuro, to introduce into his pictures an ideal beauty which surpasses that of nature, and at the very first glance enchants even the initiated; making them forget all that they have seen of the rare and the beautiful before. The St. Jerome, now in the academy of Parma, has more especially been honoured with these eulogiums. It is related of Algarotti, that, on observing this picture, he was for preferring it to every other, and could not refrain from apostrophizing Coreggio, and exclaiming:—Tu solo mi piaci!—"Thou alone pleasest me!" Annibal Carracci himself, at sight of this picture and certain others by the same hand, protests, in a letter to his cousin Lodovico, that he would not give them in exchange for the St. Cecilia of Raphael, which was then and still is at Bologna. And, to say the truth, the art of painting, which Michael Angelo had carried to the highest pitch of sublimity, Raphael to the highest pitch of expression and natural grace, and Titian to the last perfection of colouring, received from Coreggio (in the opinion at least of Mengs) a combination of excellences that rendered it complete in all its parts; adding to the sublime and the natural a certain elegance, and, as we may say, a taste directed at once to please the eye and content the heart of the spectator.

Design.—In design, Correggio did not attain the same profound knowledge as Buonarroti; yet even in this he displayed so much grandeur and taste, that the Caracci themselves took him for their model. I am aware that Algarotti does not think him always correct in the drawing of his outlines; but at the same time I am not ignorant that Mengs has defended him with much warmth from this charge. In his design we do not find that variety of lines that we meet with in Raphael's works and the remains of antiquity; for he did his utmost to avoid right lines and angles, adopting rather a continuous undulation of lines, sometimes convex, sometimes concave: nevertheless, some will have it that the gracefulness of his paintings in great measure consists in this very peculiarity; so that Mengs, uncertain what decision to come to, at one time commends him for it, at another, excuses him. He adopted this same measure for the design of his draperies, in which he paid more attention to the general masses than to the particular folds; so being the first to make the drapery enter into the real spirit of the composition both in point of contrast and arrangement, thus opening a new path to give it effect in works on a large scale. His youthful and infantine heads are more especially celebrated; smiling, as they do, with such an air of nature and simplicity, that they enchant the spectator, and force him to smile along with them. Owing to the incredible variety of foreshortenings he introduces, there is not one of his figures that has not something in it of novelty; there is scarcely a head that is not foreshortened as if seen from a point of view above or below it; scarcely a hand, I had almost said, or a whole figure, that he does not bend with a degree of grace of which there is no other example. In the art of foreshortening figures for ceilings, a task which Raphael seems to have shunned, he overcame some difficulties that still remained after the time of Mantegna; so that this branch of perspective was by his means brought to perfection.

Colouring.—With this elegance and gracefulness of design his colouring also corresponds; insomuch that Giulio Romano asserted it was the best he had ever met with; nor did he feel hurt, when the Duke of Mantua, intending to make a present of some pictures to Charles V., employed Correggio to execute them instead of himself. A similar panegyric is bestowed upon him by Lomazzo, where he affirms that he might be considered as a unique rather than as a rare example among colourists. No other painter ever bestowed so much pains upon the preparation of his canvass, upon which, after he had covered it with a composition of chalk, he painted, as we have already said, without stint either in the quantity to the quality of his colours. In the thick laying on of his colours (impasto) he approaches the manner of Giorgione, in their tint he resembles Titian; but, in the opinion of Mengs, he displays greater experience in their gradation. In his colouring, moreover, he introduced a lucid appearance which we rarely find in that of others; we may almost fancy ourselves looking at objects in a mirror; and when, at even, other pictures begin to fade upon the eye for want of light, his paintings become in some way more vivid; seeming, like stars, to overcome the darkness of the air. Of that varnish, for which Apelles is so highly applauded by Pliny, we can either form no idea at all from modern painting, or, if we can form some idea of it, it is to Correggio that we are indebted for it. There have been those who could sometimes have wished for greater delicacy in his fleshes; though every one must acknowledge that he contrived to vary them admirably according to the age and the subject; imparting to them a degree of softness, juiciness, and life, that makes them look like nature itself.

Chiaroscuro.—But his real forte, his distinguishing merit, his true pre-eminence above every other artist of whom we have any knowledge, consists in his happy management of light and shade. As nature herself does not shake every object with the same strong light, but varies it according to the superficies, the opposition, and the distance of the object; so also did Coreggio contrive to diversify it, heightening or diminishing it by so almost insensible gradation,—a point so indispensable in aërial perspective, (in which he attained the highest excellence) and so conducive to the general harmony. He pursued the same plan in some degree in his shadows; so delicately representing in each the reflection of the adjacent colour, that notwithstanding his lavish introduction of the darker tints, there is nothing of sameness in them; all is agreeably diversified. His merit in this respect is more particularly conspicuous in his Night,* in the Dresden gallery, as well as in the Magdalene, of the same gallery, represented reclining in a cave—a small picture, but in the catalogue valued at twenty-seven thousand crowns. By means of his chiaroscuro, he not only imparted an incomparable degree of roundness and softness to his figures, but diffused over the whole composition a degree of taste till then unknown; disposing the masses of his lights and shades in a manner perfectly natural in reality, though in appearance wholly ideal. To this degree of perfection he attained by pursuing

* Others have, with more propriety, called this picture The Dawn of Day.

the very same path that had been trodden by Michael Angelo—by making models in wax and chalk.

Invention—Composition—Expression.—In every other branch of painting he highly distinguished himself, though not equally in them all. His inventions were happy; except that he sometimes impaired the unity of the action by introducing different passages of the same story. Thus, in the story of Marsyas, in the Litta palace at Milan, we find expressed in different groups—his contest with Apollo—Minerva consigning him over to punishment—and the punishment itself. We may observe the same repetition in the story of Leda, painted for Charles V.; where the Swan is twice introduced gradually familiarizing himself with her, till in the third group he enjoys her. For the rest, his pictures in general have some affinity with the poems of Anacreon, in which Cupids, and, in sacred subjects, Cherubs, are seen engaged in the most winning actions: thus, in the picture of St. George, we find them disporting about the helmet and sword of the Saint; in the St. Jerome, we see an angel drawing our Saviour's attention to the writings of that great Doctor of Holy Church; while another applies to his nostrils the uncovered box of ointment of the Magdalen. Of his skill in composition, we have a proof in the cupola, in which we have more than once offered our tribute of admiration, where the architecture would seem to have been accommodated to the painting, not the painting to the architecture. He was fond of contrast, not only in different figures, but in the different parts of the same figure; yet he did not affect contrast, or carry it to that excess which afterwards prevailed, to the prejudice both of decorum and truth. His powers of expression were perhaps unexampled in subjects of a tender nature; as in the Magdalene just mentioned, who, in the act of kissing the feet of the Infant Jesus, is made to assume a look and demeanour expressive of the varied beauties scattered here and there in the works of other artists, as Mengs has at large observed—a picture, of which we may fairly say with Catullus, "Omnibus una omnes surripuit veneres." In the Dead Christ, too, at Parma, he succeeded to admiration in expressing the passion of grief, and of diversifying it according to the subject; making it the most affecting in the Magdalene, the most profound in the Virgin, while in the third figure it assumes a more moderate character. If he did not often undertake to express the fiercer passions, it was not because he wanted the power; in his Martyrdom of S. Placido, there is an executioner represented with so much truth, that Domenichino avowedly imitated it in his celebrated picture of St. Agnes.

Keeping and Erudition.—Lastly, in his sacred pieces, we have nothing more to wish for in the way of keeping: in his stories from profane fable he might have improved it, had he, like Raphael and more modern artists, adhered closely to the models of antiquity. In his Leda, Juno has the air of a woman advanced in years, who, full of spite and jealousy, watches the clandestine amours of Jupiter: there is nothing of the antique about her either in feature or accompaniments: and hence, in the descriptions of this picture, this figure is considered as a cypher. In the story of Marsyas, too, neither has Marsyas himself any thing about him of the Faun, nor has Minerva her aegis or any of her usual attributes, nor has Apollo either the face or the figure usually given to him now-a-days; while in his hand he holds a fiddle instead of a lyre. From hence we might deduce another argument to prove that Correggio never visited Rome, where even indifferent painters, by the help of those remains of antiquity with which that city abounds, learn to avoid such defects. They are, however, but trifling blemishes after all; nay, they may even be considered favourable to Correggio's fame, if they serve to make us still more certain, that the merit of his admirable style is all his own, without being attributable to the examples of a multitude of other artists. Regarded in this light, he almost appears to be something more than man; and, as Annibal Caracci observed, compared with him, Parmigianino and other painters of the same stamp dwindle into insignificance. The works of this great man become continually more and more scarce in Italy, in consequence of the great repute in which they are held, and the high prices at which they are purchased, by foreigners. Their place, however, is supplied by many old copies, especially of the smaller pictures; such as the Nuptials of St. Catherine, the Magdalene in Repose, the Flight of the Young Man; pieces already mentioned: to these we may add, Christ's Prayer in the Garden, of which the original is in the Escurial, and that other picture at Dresden, called the Zingherina. Among these old copies the most esteemed are those executed by Schedone, Lelio da Novellara, Girolamo da Carpi, and the Caracci; the latter of whom, by long practice in copying Correggio's works, made very near approaches to the originals, though always more so in design than in skill and delicacy of colouring.

Thus far have I described at one and the same time the style of Antonio Allegri and that of his school; not because any one has ever yet equalled or even approached him, but because all of them held nearly the same maxims; though not always without introducing certain others. The distinguishing feature of the Parmesan school, called also by way of eminence the Lombard school, is foreshortening; as the expression of the nerves and muscles is of the Florentine: nor is it of much importance to add, that here too the foreshortened style was by some carried to affectation and excess, just as the anatomical was at Florence: to imitate well is every where found to be a difficult task. Among the characteristics of this school we may also notice a closer attention to chiaroscuro and the disposition of the drapery than to the representation of the human frame, in which few are really thought to have evinced much merit. Their contours are ample, their heads not so much ideal as selected from among the people of that state, in whom they are usually found to be well rounded, high coloured, and not unfrequently possessed of those features and that joyousness which in Coreggio's works pass for original.*

* Among Coreggio's more eminent followers we may notice his son Pomponio Allegri, Fra Maria Rondani, Michelangiolo Anselmi, Bernardino Gatti, and Giorgio Gandini.

PARMIGIANINO.

The life of Francesco Mazzuola, called Il Parmigianino, has been written by the Padre Affò. That biographer is of opinion that he was not the scholar of Coreggio, but of his two uncles; in whose studio he must have painted that Baptism of Christ, which is now in the possession of the Conte Sanvitali, and which, for a boy of fourteen, (Francesco's age at the time,) is an admirable performance. The same biographer remarks, that at sight of Coreggio's works, Francesco became one of his followers; and to this period are referred certain pictures of his which betray a palpable imitation of that master's style; such as a Holy Family, in the possession of the President Bertioli, and a S. Bernardino in that of the Padri Osservanti at Parma. Indeed the mere circumstance of Francesco's having been chosen, together with Rondani and Anselmi, to paint a chapel near the cupola of Coreggio, proves that, like the other two, he must have acquired a style somewhat analogous to his, and have evinced some degree of docility in following his directions. He was, however, too conscious of his own powers to rest satisfied at being second in one style, while he found himself able to become first in another; and such, in fact, he afterwards became; for, owing to the continued procrastination of the aforementioned work, he made the tour of Italy; and having seen Giulio at Mantua, and Raphael at Rome, he formed a style which passes for original. It is at once grand, noble, and dignified; not prodigal of figures, but making a few produce a powerful effect even in a large picture: as in the S. Rocco at S. Petronio of Bologna, or that celebrated chiaroscuro the Moses at the Steccata of Parma.

Nevertheless, the distinguishing characteristic and proper province of this artist, is grace; insomuch that it was a common saying at Rome, that the spirit of Raphael had passed into him. To this object he directed all his efforts. In his designs we are continually meeting with repetitions of the same figure—trials which he had made in order to attain the highest grace in the form and attitudes of his figures, and in the lightness of his drapery, in which latter he was eminently successful. Algarotti was of opinion, that in his heads he sometimes overstepped the mark, and sunk into affectation; a critique for which Agostino Caracci paved the way, when he required in the painter 'un po' di grazia del Parmigianino;' a little of Parmigianino's grace, not the whole of it, because it appeared to him to be carried too far.

It was, too, according to others, owing to this over-studiousness of grace that he sometimes dealt in proportions of too great length, not only as regards the stature of the figures themselves, but the fingers and the neck; as in the celebrated Madonna of the Pitti palace, which from this defect is usually called the Madonna of the Long Neck (Madonna del Collo Lungo); but in this he was not without his apologists. This gracefulness of style is moreover promoted even by his colouring; which is, for the most part, of a quiet, sober, and subdued tone, as though it were loth to present itself to the eye with too much vivacity. If we abide by Albani's decision, Parmigianino was not very studious of expression, of which he has left but few examples; though, in fact, that very grace that animates his infantine and other delicate figures, either deserves the name of expression; or, if that quality require the passions solely, it sufficiently well supplies its place. It is, indeed, on account of this grace that we so readily overlook his errors, and suffer even his defects to pass for merits.

It would seem that he was somewhat slow of conception, and accustomed to shape the whole picture in his imagination before he put his hand to the pencil; but that he was afterwards quick in execution. In his works we observe some strokes so bold and free, that Albani calls them divine.

and asserts, that it was to his great practice in the art of design that he owed this inimitable facility; which, however, in him was not dissociated from diligence and high finish. His works do not all exhibit the same full body of colouring, nor all produce the same effect; yet there are some of them, which their author painted con amore, that have even been ascribed to Correggio. Such is the Cupid constructing his Bow, at whose feet are two infantine figures, the one laughing, the other crying; of which, besides the one in the Imperial gallery, there are various other duplicates; so much did it take the fancy either of the author himself or of some other artist. With regard to this picture, I follow the opinion of Vasari, supported as it is by the Padre Affò, and many other connoisseurs with whom I have conversed on the subject; for the rest, Boschini calls this Cupid as indisputably a Correggio as either the Ganymede or the Leda, mentioned in the same controversy (p. 303); an opinion which has been, and still is countenanced by many others.

Parmigianino's smaller pictures, portraits, youthful heads, and sacred figures, are not very rare, and some of them are found repeated in various places. The one most frequently to be met with in different collections, is a picture of the Virgin with the Infant Jesus and St. John; to which are added, St. Catherine and St. Zacharias, or some such old head, placed close to the former. This painting was formerly to be seen in the Farnese gallery at Parma; and such a painting, or one very much resembling it, may still be seen in the Florentine and Capitoline galleries; in those of the Corsini, Borghese, and Albani princes at Rome; and, at Parma, in that of the Abate Mazza, as well as elsewhere; nor is it easy to believe they can all be original, of however old a date. Copious compositions of his are rarely to be met with; such as the Christ preaching to the Multitude, to be seen in one of the ducal apartments at Colorno, and one of the greatest jewels of that delightful villa. His altar-pieces are not very numerous; nor is any one of them more highly prized than the S. Margherita at Bologna. It is a picture that abounds with figures, and one which the Carracci thought they could never sufficiently study and admire; while Guido, in a sort of transport, even preferred it to the St. Cecilia of Raphael. Another of his more remarkable works is the fresco which he commenced at the Steccata, where, besides the Moses in chiaroscuro, he painted an Adam and Eve and some Virtues, without, however, completing the work, for which he had been paid. In consequence of having left this work in an unfinished state, Francesco was thrown into prison, and afterwards lived in exile at Casale, where he died at the age of thirty-seven, the age of his favourite Raphael. He was heralded as one of the first luminaries not only of the art of painting, but of the art of engraving on copper.*

CREMONESE SCHOOL.

EPOCH I.

THE OLD MASTERS.

I HAVE never read the lives of Bernardino and the rest of the Campi, without desiring I could discover in the school of Cremona, which they founded, the first sketch of that which the Caracci afterwards established at Bologna. In each of those cities one single family formed the project of striking out a new style of painting, which should partake of the manner of all the different schools of Italy, without directly borrowing from any; in each of those cities there proceeded from one single family such a number of eminent mas-

* [illegible]

ters, that, partly by their own efforts, partly by means of their scholars, they not only embellished their country with their works, but did honour to the art itself by their example, and to its annals by their name. That the school of Cremona did not in the sequel come up to that of Bologna in merit and in fame—that it did not last so long as the *Carracceschi*—that this latter succeeded in some measure in accomplishing what the other had but attempted; all this may be imputed to a variety of causes. For the present, however, I proceed, according to my usual rout, to notice the first germs of this school; nor need we, in our search after them, go farther than that magnificent cathedral, which was commenced in 1107, and, at the earliest opportunity, decorated both with sculpture and painting. In each of these branches there are specimens well worth the attention of the antiquarian whose object it is to ascertain by what means, and by what steps, the arts gradually revived in Italy. The sculpture, indeed, presents us with nothing but what we may also witness at Verona, Crema, and other places; whereas, the paintings still in being on the two side aisles are perfectly unique, and worth the trouble of a close inspection, seeing that the figures are small, and that there is a deficiency of light. The subjects are taken from holy writ; the design is beyond measure dry, the colouring strong, the drapery wholly new; except in so far as some of them continue to be met with even now-a-days in masquerades, or on the Italian stage. There are also edifices given merely in outline, as in some of the older wood-cuts; and there are also written characters to explain the principal figures, as we sometimes meet with in the older mosaics, when the eye, not yet accustomed to the contemplation of historical pieces, stood in need of such explanations. There is here, however, nothing to remind us of the Greek mosaics; every thing is Italian, novel, and national. The written characters leave us in no doubt as to whether we should ascribe these works to Giotto's or to the preceding age; but the figures prove that their author was indebted neither to Giotto nor Cimabue for any portion of his acquirements.*

* [illegible]

CREMONESE SCHOOL.

EPOCH II.

CAMILLO BOCCACCINO, IL SOIARO, THE CAMPI.

The noble cathedral of Cremona, and still more the church of St. Sigismund, which had been erected by Francesco Sforza at a short distance from the city, contributed not a little to the advancement even of these more modern artists— Camillo Boccaccino, Soiaro, and the Campi; who, as well as their descendants, painting there in competition with each other, converted it into a sort of school of the fine arts. There we may in some sort trace the order in which those masters followed each other; their various merits; their predominating style, which was that of Coreggio; their different modes of modifying it; and their remarkable talent for frescos. With these they

he was, according to Pascoli's account; less symmetrical in point of composition, less graceful as regards the air of the heads, and less forcible in chiaroscuro; but richer in the drapery, more varied in the colouring, more spirited in the attitudes, and perhaps not less harmonious nor less attractive in the landscapes and architectural embellishments.

embellished not only their churches, but, in every street, covering with them the façades of palaces and private dwellings, they imparted to their native place a brilliancy of exterior that failed not to excite the admiration of strangers: insomuch that on their arrival at Cremona, they were apt to fancy they were contemplating a city on the eve of a rejoicing, and decked out, as it were, for some gay and splendid pageant.

Camillo Boccaccino is the greatest genius of the school. Initiated in the old maxims of the art adopted by his father, he contrived, without enjoying a long life, to hit upon a style in which the graceful and the vigorous were so happily blended together, that it would be hard to say in which of those two properties he succeeded best. There are pictures of his still in being, on the cupola, the principal recess, and the sides of the larger altar, in the church of St Sigismund. The most celebrated of these pieces are the four Evangelists, represented in a sitting posture, with the exception of St John, who is standing, and who, with body bent in an attitude of wonder, forms a curve of contrary flexure compared with that of the ceiling—a figure equally famed for the design and the perspective. It seems almost incredible that a mere youth could, without frequenting the school of Correggio, so well have imitated his style, and have carried it even farther than himself in so short a space of time; for this work, which exhibits so thorough a knowledge of perspective and foreshortening, was executed in 1537.

At Cremona, as well as elsewhere, much applause has also been lavished on the two framed figures above-mentioned—the one representing the Resurrection of Lazarus, the other the story of the Woman taken in Adultery, surrounded with beautiful borders exhibiting a crowd of sportive Cherubs that look as though they were alive,—one of them holding a mitre, another a censer, a third some other sacred vessel. In these two pieces therefore, as well as the surrounding borders, the figures are all of them disposed and turned in such a manner, that we can hardly in a single instance distinguish the eyes of any of them,—a whimsical procedure, to say the truth, that ought never to be imitated. Camillo's object was to convince his rivals, that his figures did not owe their attractions, as they were wont to affirm, solely to the vivacity of the eyes, but to the merits of all the other parts. And, in fact, these figures, notwithstanding their peculiar posture, are highly pleasing for the design, the variety and beauty of the attitudes, the foreshortenings, the truth of the colouring, and the strength of the chiaroscuro, which I suspect he derived from Pordenone, and which, by comparison, makes the pictures of the Campi at the same place look as if deficient in relief.

Bernardino Gatti has already been noticed among the artists of the Parmesan school;* I must now at least briefly notice him among the more eminent of those of Cremona. Cremona possesses a considerable number of Soiaro's pictures, from those that he executed in early youth down to those that he painted in extreme old age, when, having now attained his eightieth year and become afflicted with palsy, he painted with the left hand. It was then, however, that he painted for the cathedral his picture of the Assumption—a picture fifty palms high—which, though left unfinished in consequence of its author's death, is, as Lanzi has justly observed, a most admirable performance. Gervasio Gatti il Soiaro is also celebrated in story: he was the nephew of Bernardino, who led him, while yet a youth, to that same fountain-head at which he himself had slaked his thirst—Correggio's works at Parma, which he taught him to copy and design.

The Campi.—These were four in number; all of them were indefatigable in their profession; all of them lived to a good old age. These latter

* In the present [illegible]

been those who have styled them the Vasaris and the Zuccaris of Lombardy; a comparison which has some degree of fairness in it, if we confine it only to the grand scale of their larger compositions, as well as to the great number of their other works; but more of injustice, if, as would seem to be implied, we are to extend it also to a desire on their part to paint a great deal, rather than to paint well. Giulio and Bernardino—the more eminent of the Campi—if they sometimes despatched their works in too hasty and negligent a manner, this did not often happen; and much even of this may be attributed to their coadjutors. For the rest, they usually paid due attention to the accuracy of their design and the good quality of their colours; whence their tints still retain their freshness, while, in the works of the followers of Vasari and the Zuccari, the colours, having in great part faded, stand in need of being refreshed, and, as it were, restored to life again, by the hands of modern artists.

GIULIO CAMPI.

Giulio Campi may be considered as the Lodovico Caracci of his school. The elder brother of Antonio and Vincenzo, and Bernardino's coadjutor, or, at least, his master, he conceived the design of forming a style which should combine the perfections of various others. His father, from whom he had received some instructions during his earlier years, not conceiving himself equal to the task of completing his education, sent him to the school of Giulio Romano, who was then at Milan. Accordingly, under Giulio Romano he laid the foundation of his style; and from him derived that grandiosity of design, that skill in the representation of the naked figure, that variety and fertility of fancy, those magnificent architectural embellishments, and that universality of talent, which enabled him to handle any subject with success. This admirable acquirement he carried still further on occasion of his visit to Rome, where he studied the works of Raphael and the remains of antiquity; and where he copied with singular fidelity the relievos on Trajan's Pillar, works which have ever been looked upon as a school of ancient art open to the student even of our own days.

Whether it was at Mantua or elsewhere I know not, but this I do know, that he studied the works of Titian, and that he was not inferior to any other stranger in his imitations of them. With regard to two others whom he took for his models, he had no need to go beyond the confines of his own country in quest of them: these were Pordenone and Soiaro; whose style, according to Vasari, he adopted before he knew or imitated Giulio Romano. To such preparatory steps, to which we must add the copying whatever of Raphael's or Coreggio's works came in his way, was he indebted for that style which exhibits vestiges of the manner of so many different artists.

Giulio Campi, however, was not so wholly intent on imitating the great masters, as to be unmindful of nature. On the contrary, nature was the object which he, as well as the rest of the Campi, (to whom he acted as preceptor,) constantly had in view. In their works we continually meet with heads, especially female heads, copied from such as Cremona presented to their observation. The colouring of these heads approximates to that of Paolo Veronese. In the distribution of their colours, the Campi follow, with little exception, the method most general in Italy previous to the time of the Carracci; but in their mode of applying and giving vigour to them, they evince a gracefulness peculiar to themselves, which Scaramuccia looked upon as altogether original. Hence, on observing merely their colouring and the style of their heads, it is not so easy to distinguish one of the Campi from another; but on observing their design, there is less difficulty in making such distinction. Giulio surpasses the rest of the Campi in grandeur of style; and is the one who aims most at appearing skilled in the anatomy of the human frame and the management of light and shade. In chasteness of design he excels his two brothers, but is in this respect inferior to Bernardino.

ANTONIO CAMPI.

Antonio Campi was instructed by his brother both in painting and architecture, which latter he cultivated more assiduously than Giulio. He also cultivated the art of modelling and that of copper-plate engraving, and ranks moreover among the chroniclers of his native place, of which he published an account, enriched with a number of engravings, in the year 1585. He is therefore among the Campi what Agostino is among the Carracci; an artist of multifarious accomplishments and not deficient in polite literature. The master to whom he most usually looked up to as a model, was Correggio; and the part in which he chiefly aimed at distinguishing himself, was grace. As regards the colouring, he frequently attained his object in this respect; less frequently, however, in point of design; where, from his eagerness to attain the graceful, he sometimes degenerated into the slender, while at other times, by seeking to display his skill in foreshortening, he introduces it out of place. In subjects of a robust character he betrays still greater mannerism; and now and then inclines to heaviness; a defect which may, in like manner, have arisen from his eagerness to imitate the grandiosity of Correggio, which is perhaps more difficult of imitation than even his gracefulness. Many of these faults, however, as well as the inaccuracy of design of which he was occasionally guilty, may admit of palliation as being imputable to his assistants, of whom he had a great number in the vast works that he executed. The same excuse, however, cannot be pleaded for the crowded composition observable in some of his works; nor for the introduction of caricatures into his sacred pieces; which is something like jesting at an unseasonable time. In a word, he was endowed with a comprehensive, vigorous, and resolute genius; but a genius that required restraint; and in this respect, as well as in what relates generally to a profound knowledge of the

ter, we should do wrong to compare him to Agostino Carracci.

Vincenzio Campi.—From Antonio Campi we learn Vincenzio was the youngest of the three brothers; and we learn from others that he was the constant companion of his brothers' labours, though about as fit to be compared with them as was Francesco Carracci to be compared to his brothers, Annibale and Agostino. His portraits, however, and fruit-pieces, (which latter he represented with a good deal of truth and nature in cabinet pictures by no means rare at Cremona,) are much esteemed. His historical pieces are, perhaps, equal to those of his brothers' in point of colouring, but inferior to them in invention and design.

BERNARDINO CAMPI.

Bernardino Campi, probably a relative of the three Campi, of whom we have just made such honourable mention, is, with regard to them, what Annibale is with regard to the rest of the Carracci. Having imbibed the rudiments of art from the elder of the Campi, he entered into the same views of forming a style that might partake of various others; and in a short time emulated, and in the opinion of some, surpassed his master. At first, in compliance with his father's wishes, he had followed the trade of a goldsmith; but subsequently, at sight of two of Raphael's tapestries that had been copied by Giulio Campi, he resolved to change his profession; and, placing himself under the instruction, first of Campi, at Cremona, next of Ippolito Costa, at Mantua, he began, when no more than nineteen years old, to profess the art of painting, and might, at that early age, have been considered a proficient in it. At Mantua he had made himself acquainted with Giulio Romano and his school; and there is reason to think that his ideas expanded on witnessing Giulio's performances, and that he thence acquired a taste for great undertakings: still, however, his darling model was Raphael; the paintings, the designs, and engravings from Raphael's works, were the object of his delight; while, with regard to Giulio and others, I suspect he emulated those properties only in which he seemed to recognize his favourite Raphael. At Mantua also he studied Titian's eleven Caesars; and having copied them, he added a twelfth, so exactly corresponding in style, that it looked more like an original than an imitation. He was, moreover, by the liberality of a certain patron of his, enabled to visit Parma, Modena, and Reggio, in order to make himself acquainted with Coreggio's style; and how much he profited by the excursion, the paintings at St. Sigismund afford sufficient proof. Out of these elements, and others that he met with in his native place, he formed a style which may rank among the most novel to be found among imitators. The kind of imitation in which he deals is not, like that of some others, palpable; it resembles Sannazaro's imitation of the best Latin poets, who, while every one of his lines is imbued with it, yet contrives to make every line wholly and properly his own. And as Virgil was Sannazaro's favourite model, so, among the variety of models that he imitated, the one in which he most delighted and which he chiefly followed, was Raphael; and well had it been for him, had he seen Rome itself and the original works of that consummate master. This disadvantage he compensated as he best could, adopting certain principles founded in simplicity and nature, which distinguished him from the rest of his school. Compared with the rest of the Campi, he appears the most timid but the most correct; he has less of grandeur than Giulio Campi, but more of ideal beauty, and makes a more forcible appeal to the heart. In the length of his proportions he resembles Antonio rather than Giulio Campi, but in no other respect; excepting that sometimes, as in the Assumption at the cathedral, he seems to border on dryness, in order to avoid falling into mannerism.

CREMONESE SCHOOL.

EPOCH III.

THE SCHOOL OF THE CAMPI DECLINES—TROTTI AND OTHERS SUSTAIN IT.

From the sketch that I have just taken, it is no hard matter to perceive that the school of the Campi was a sort of rough draught of that of the Carracci; nor is it difficult to understand why, while they both proceeded on the same plan, the former should have been less successful than the latter. The Carracci all three of them excelled in design, and always aimed at giving proofs of it: they were, moreover, of one mind and confined to one spot, whence they invariably afforded each other mutual assistance; besides this, they kept in constant operation a school, of which the object was, not so much to study the different manners of different artists, as to enter philosophically into the various effects of nature, in order that their works might be immediately, not distantly, related to her. The Campi, on the contrary, neither uniformly aspired after excellence, nor lived together, nor ever united in forming a school on such a systematic and well-regulated plan: each of them not only dwelt alone, but kept a separate school; teaching his scholars, if I mistake not, rather to imitate himself than to penetrate into the true principles of the art. Hence it came to pass, that while Domenichino, Guido, Guercino, and other followers of the Caracci, started up with a variety of styles distinguished for novelty and originality, the scholars of the Campi were remarkable only for imitating as closely as they could the painters of their native place, either individually or collectively. Nay, further, since man is every where alike, the same thing that occurred in the other schools of Italy occurred also here,—their successors having acquired some degree of ability in imitating those that preceded them, gave way to negligence in the execution of their works; and while the latter drew almost every thing from nature, preparing cartoons, making wax models, and paying the utmost attention to the disposition of the drapery, and every other circumstance; the former contented themselves with preparing an imperfect sketch of their work and copying a few heads from nature, executing the rest in a more mechanical manner, and as best suited their convenience. Thus, by degrees, even this illustrious school degenerated; and at the time, too, that the scholars of the Procaccini were pursuing the very same method at Milan. Hence, during the seventeenth century, Lombardy was overrun with servile imitators, (settarj) in comparison of whom the followers of Zuccari might be called eminent painters.

Trotti.—Of all Bernardino Campi's scholars, his greatest favourite was Gio. Batista Trotti. This latter happening to be employed at Parma in company with Agostino Carracci, and being at that court more applauded than his rival, was denominated by Agostino a hard bone—mal osso—which they had given him to gnaw. Hence he ever afterwards retained the nickname of Malosso, a name which he willingly adopted, with which he subscribed his works, and which he transmitted to his nephew. Thus it would seem that he took for praise, what Agostino had meant for censure; the latter complaining by that expression that a man of inferior merit should have been preferred before himself. And, to say the truth, Malosso was not a match for his competitor either in design or solidity of taste: his works, however, exhibited certain attractive qualities well suited to gain him a powerful party, and enable him to make head against every other artist. To Bernardino's style he adhered only in his earlier performances; subsequently he attentively studied Coreggio's works; but still more did he look up to Soiaro as his model; whose gay, open, and brilliant style, remarkable for the variety of its foreshortenings and the vivacity of its attitudes, he imitated in the greater part of his works. He even carried this imitation too far, frequently indulging to excess in whites and other bright colours, without sufficiently modifying them with those of a darker hue; whence I have sometimes heard his paintings compared to those on china, and charged with want of relief, or, as Baldinucci has it, with something of a hard dry manner. His heads are very beautiful; exhibiting, like Soiaro's, a graceful roundness and a fascinating smile; but he is too fond of repeating them; introducing even into the same piece heads of which the features, the colouring, and expression, are very nearly the same. This defect we can impute only to his excessive haste; for assuredly he could not be charged with any want of fancy.

Trotti formed no small number of pupils, who flourished about the year 1600, and were very tenacious of his manner; though, in process of time, the mode of laying on the grounds having, throughout the whole of Italy, undergone a change for the worse, and the age giving the preference to a style of a more sombre character, those pupils began to depart from the brightness which formed the distinguishing feature of his works.

MILANESE SCHOOL.

EPOCH I.

THE OLD MASTERS, TILL THE APPEARANCE OF DA VINCI.

If, in our account of each of the Italian schools, we have made a point of going back to the dark ages, and thence coming gradually down to more polished times, Milan, the capital of Lombardy and the residence of the Lombard kings, presents us with an epoch which, from its importance and the grandeur of its monuments, must not be passed over in silence. When the kingdom of Italy passed from the Goths to the Lombards, the arts, which invariably follow in the train of Fortune, transferred their chief seat from Ravenna to Milan, Monza, and Pavia. In each of these places there exist even now some vestiges of that style, which, from the country and the period, is still denominated Lombard; just as, in the science of diplomacy, the name Lombard is still applied to certain written characters peculiar to that age, or rather to those ages; inasmuch as, even after the Lombards were expelled from Italy, the same character was employed in inscriptions and writings throughout great part of it. The style of which we are speaking, as displayed in the works of that age, whether in metal or marble, is rude and uncouth beyond all former example; and is seen more frequently, as well as to more advantage, in the representation of monsters (both birds and beasts) than of human figures. At the cathedral, the church of St. Michael's, that of St. John's at Pavia, we see, on the friezes over the doors, animals linked together in various ways, sometimes in a posture not unnatural, sometimes with the head turned backward; and within the same churches, as well as certain others, we meet with capitals of pillars decorated with similar figures; sometimes with the addition of historical pieces presenting figures of men, I had almost said, of another species—so little resemblance do they bear to the human race. The same perverted taste pervaded the territories over which the Lombard Dukes bore sway; such as Friuli, which still retains many monuments of this barbarous style. At Cividale there is a marble altar commenced by the Duke Pemmone, and completed by his son Ratchis, both of whom lived during the eighth century; the bas-reliefs represent—Our Saviour seated amidst various Angels—the Epiphany—and the Visitation of the Blessed Virgin. It would seem impossible that any thing could exceed the rudeness of these figures; and yet whoever chooses to examine on the spot the frieze over one of the doors, or the capitals of the pillars, of S. Celso at Milan—works of the tenth century—will acknowledge that it was possible to carry the depravation of art still further, when to the rude was added the ridiculous, and when abortive figures were produced, all hands and heads, with legs and feet ill calculated to support them. Of this character there are very many statues at Verona and elsewhere. There are nevertheless monuments which will not permit us to maintain, as a system, that there were in Italy at that time no vestiges whatever of the correct style of the ancients.*

* Lanzi here proceeds to notice a few anonymous pictures to be seen at Monza, Pavia, Bellano, and Milan, of a date anterior to Giotto, who executed some few works at the latter place about the year 1335. He observes, too, that shortly afterwards Giotto's most distinguished scholar, Stefano Fiorentino, was invited to Milan by Matteo Visconti. He then goes on to notice various old Milanese painters, till we come to Vincenzio Foppa, who flourished about 1450, and who, he says, may be more correctly looked upon as the founder of the Milanese school. Contemporary at this period, the most distinguished of those recorded under this first epoch, are,—Bernardino da Trevio, Bramante Lazzari, Bramantino, Agostino di Milano, Giovanni Donato Montorfano, and Civerchio.

MILANESE SCHOOL.

EPOCH II.

DA VINCI ESTABLISHES A SCHOOL OF DESIGN AT MILAN. PUPILS OF THAT SCHOOL AND OF THE BEST NATIVE ARTISTS DOWN TO THE TIME OF GAUDENZIO.

In treating of the Florentine school, we gave a compendious account of Leonardo da Vinci's education in the art of painting, of his style, and of his residence in various cities, amongst which we took occasion to notice Milan, and the academy that he opened there. The years that Leonardo spent at Milan were perhaps the most tranquil of his life, and certainly the most conducive to the advancement of art. It was chiefly through his means that the Milanese school became one of the most observant of keeping of any in Italy. Mengs has already remarked, that in the management of strong chiaroscuro no one surpassed Da Vinci. He taught his scholars to look upon light as though it had been a gem; not to diffuse it indiscriminately, but to reserve it for those parts where it would produce the greatest effect. Hence it is that, in his paintings, and those of his more distinguished followers, we meet with that strong relief, owing to which the pictures themselves, but more especially the heads, seem almost to start from the canvass.

A considerable period had now elapsed since painters had begun to pay more attention to the delicacies and minutiæ of art; a point in which Botticelli, Mantegna, and others, had already extorted the praise of their contemporaries. But as minuteness is incompatible with sublimity, it would but ill accord with that elevation in which consists the perfection of art. Leonardo, as it appears to me, was the first who succeeded in reconciling those two extremes. Whenever he took the pains to produce a finished performance, he not only imparted the last perfection to the heads, imitating the sparkling of the eyes, the setting on of the hair, the pores of the skin, and even the pulsation of the arteries; but also drew with the utmost minuteness every garment and every ornament. In his landscapes, too, there is not a single plant or a single leaf of a tree that is not copied from the choicest nature; while to the leaves themselves is given a flexibility and movement admirably suited to represent them as agitated by the wind. But, as Mengs himself has observed, while he thus attended even to little things, he laid the foundation of a more elevated style, and studied, more profoundly than any other artist on record, that most philosophical and sublime walk of art, expression; in which respect he may even be said to have paved the way for Raphael himself. Never was there any one more curious in investigating, more diligent in observing, or more prompt in catching the various expressions of the passions, as indicated either by the features or the gestures. He used to haunt the more frequented places and the theatres, where man puts forth his greatest energy; and there, in a little sketch-book, which he always had about him, he copied the attitudes of which he was in quest: these he kept by him, availing himself afterwards of such of them as were of a more or less forcible expression, as occasion required, or according to the different gradations that he wished to represent. For, in the same manner as he was wont continually to heighten his shadows till he had carried them to the highest pitch, so, in compositions containing several figures, he went on heightening their effect till he had carried the different emotions of the mind, and the different gestures of the body, to the highest point of expression. The same gradation he observed with regard to grace, of which he was perhaps the earliest votary; for the painters who preceded him seem not to have discriminated between this property and beauty; and still less to have adapted it to pleasing subjects in such a way as to pass on from one degree of it to another, as was the case with Da Vinci. He observed the same rule also even in the ridiculous: making each succeeding caricature more whimsical than the preceding. Indeed, it was a saying of his, that this quality ought to be carried to such a pitch, as, if it were possible, to provoke laughter even in the dead.

The distinguishing characteristic of this incomparable artist consists in an exquisiteness of taste, of which it would be difficult to find any other example either before or since; had we not heard of that Protogenes of old, with regard to whom Apelles could discover no other means for giving himself the preference to him, save his excessive diligence. And, in fact, even Da Vinci was not always sufficiently mindful of that ne quid nimis in which the perfection of human things consists. Phidias himself, said Cicero, had in his mind's eye a more beautiful Minerva and a more majestic Jupiter, than his art was capable of creating. It is the part of a wise man to aspire to the highest excellence, but still to rest content with lower degrees of it. Da Vinci was dissatisfied with his performances unless he succeeded in imparting to them all that perfection of which he conceived them capable; and finding it impossible, after all his efforts, to arrive at such a pitch of excellence, he sometimes stopped short at the design; sometimes carried the work to a certain point, and then abandoned it; sometimes spent such a length of time upon it, that one might almost have fancied

Protogenes to have come to life again, who spent seven years upon his picture of Jalysus. But as that figure constantly unfolded fresh beauties to the admiring eyes of the spectator, so was it also, according to Lomazzo, with Da Vinci's paintings; even such of them as Vasari and others mention as unfinished.

Before we proceed further, it is the duty of a biographer, having here noticed Da Vinci's unfinished works, to put the reader in possession of the real meaning of this expression, when applied to that artist. Various works of his were no doubt left in an unfinished state, as the Epiphany in the Grand Duke's gallery at Florence, or the Holy Family in that of the Archbishop at Milan. In general, however, this expression signifies nothing more than the want of a certain last degree of finish, which the author might have given to some part of the picture; a want that cannot always be detected even by the best judges. The portrait of Mona Lisa Gioconda, for instance, on which he spent no less than four years at Florence, and which, according to Vasari, was after all left imperfect, was by Mariette, who observed it minutely in the gallery of the King of France, declared to be finished in so exquisite a manner, that it would seem impossible to have carried it further. A want of finish may be more easily recognised in other portraits of his, several of which still exist at Milan; such as one of a woman, in the possession of Prince Albani; another of a man, in the Scotti Gallarati palace; Lomazzo having remarked that, with the exception of three or four, he left the heads imperfect in all the rest. But what were imperfections and defects in him, would constitute the highest merit and the glory of numberless others.

All accounts, too, represent as an unfinished performance, that celebrated Last Supper, which he painted in the refectory of the Padri Domenicani at Milan, and yet all accounts agree in extolling it as one of the most beautiful pictures that ever proceeded from the hand of man. This picture is a compendium, not only of all that Leonardo taught in his works, but of all that he comprised within the compass of his studies. He there seized the moment best suited to give animation and interest to his subject; the moment when the Blessed Redeemer says to his disciples:—"One of you shall betray me." At these words, each of his innocent followers starts as if thunderstruck; such as are farthest off are seen interrogating their next neighbour, as though they fancied their ears must have deceived them; others, according to their different dispositions, are differently affected; one swoons away, another is lost in amazement, another springs upon his feet in indignation, another protests, with an air of genuine can-

plicity and candour that he ought to be above suspicion. Judas, in the mean time, contracts his brow; and though he counterfeits innocence, leaves us no room to doubt that he is the traitor. Da Vinci used to say, that he had meditated for a whole year how best to represent a set of features worthy of so black a heart; and that, frequenting a quarter where men of the worst character used to collect together, he there copied a head much to the purpose, adding to it, however, lineaments borrowed from various others. The like pains he took in portraying in the two Jameses a beauty of feature suited to the character of each; and having lavished his last touch of majesty on them, he left the head of Christ incomplete, as Vasari affirms; though, to Armenini, this too appeared most highly finished. The rest of the picture, the table-cloth with its folds, the various utensils, the table itself, the architectural ornaments, the distribution of the lights, the perspective of the ceiling, (which in the tapestry of St. Peter's at Rome is changed into a sort of hanging garden,) all was executed with consummate care; all was worthy of the most delicate pencil the world ever saw. Had Da Vinci but been content to paint in distemper, according to the custom of the times, the art would have been in possession of this treasure at the present day. But Da Vinci, who was always attempting new methods, painted it on a certain *imprimitura* of his own invention prepared with *distilled oils*; and to this method of his was it owing that the picture gradually peeled off from the wall; as is the case also with a Madonna painted by him in S. Onofrio at Rome, although kept under glass. Only fifty years after the execution of the Last Supper, that is to say, when Armenini saw it, it was already "half effaced;" and Scannelli, who saw it in 1642, records that "it was with difficulty the story could then be made out." It will be enough for me to add, that of the whole picture nothing now exists of Da Vinci's execution, except the heads of three of the Apostles; and of these the design, rather than the colouring, remains. Milan possesses but few of Da Vinci's works. Most of those that are pointed out as his, were painted by his scholars, though sometimes retouched by him; as the altar-piece of S. Ambrogio *ad Nemus*, a very beautiful performance. A Madonna with the Infant Jesus, at the Belgioioso d'Este palace, is considered as an indisputable work of his; as well as another picture or two in the hands of private individuals.

Of all his labours at Milan, nothing is more worthy of commemoration than the academy he founded there; for the painters it produced constitute the pride and glory of the Milanese school. They are not all equally known; and it not unfrequently happens that, both in the different galleries and churches, pictures are pointed out as belonging to Da Vinci's school, without being referred to any particular author. Their altar-pieces seldom depart much from the style of composition common at that time to every school—the Virgin with the Infant Saviour on a throne, attended by various Saints for the most part standing erect around it, and an Angel or two on the steps. Da Vinci's followers, however, were, if I mistake not, the first to bring their figures to something like a unity of action; giving them the appearance of addressing or conversing with one another. In every other respect, too, they exhibit considerable uniformity of taste; they display the same oval faces, the same simpering lips, the same fondness for precise and somewhat hard contours, the same subdued tone and harmony of colouring, the same predilection for chiaroscuro; which the less skilful among them carry to excess, while the more distinguished use it in moderation.

Cesare da Sesto.—One of those who, for a time, made the nearest approach to Da Vinci's style, was Cesare da Sesto. In the Ambrosian Library there is a head of an old man by him, in which he has admirably hit off the highly finished and lucid style of Leonardo. He passes for the most eminent of Leonardo's scholars; and is, by Lomazzo, from time to time held up as a model in design, attitude, and the art of disposing the lights. He notices an Herodias of his, of which I met with a copy in the possession of the Counsellor Pagave; and of which the countenance struck me as bearing a strong likeness to the Fornarina of Raphael.

Marco da Oggiono may be reckoned among the best of the Milanese painters. He did not confine himself to easel pictures, as was the case with the greater number of Da Vinci's scholars, who were accustomed to paint little and well; but was also eminently successful in fresco; and his works at the convent della Pace still remain unimpaired in the contours, and uninjured in the colouring. Some of these are in the church, and one very copious picture of the Crucifixion is in the refectory,—an admirable performance, whether we regard the variety, the beauty, or the vivacity of the figures. Few of the Lombard painters have attained the degree of expression we here meet with; few exhibit the same skilfulness of composition, or the same elegance of drapery. In the light elegance of his human figures, and the beauty of his horses, we recognise the scholar of Da Vinci. In another refectory—that of the Certosa at Pavia—he painted a copy of Leonardo's Last Supper; and so well did he do it, that this copy in some measure atones for the loss of the original. Milan has two other altar-pieces of his, the one at S. Paolo in Compito, the other at S. Eufemia, executed in the style already described as peculiar to the school, and of great beauty and value; but the style which he pursued in his frescos is softer and more in conformity with the modern manner.

LUINI.

It remains for us to say something of the most celebrated of Da Vinci's imitators—Bernardin Lovino, according to his own mode of spelling his name, or, according to the more commonly received method, Luini; a native of Luino, on the Lago Maggiore. Certain others of Leonardo's scholars have surpassed him in nicety of finish, or gracefulness of chiaroscuro; in which latter respect Lomazzo gives the preference to Cesar da Sesto, affirming that Luini's shadows are of a less delicate character. Notwithstanding this, taking into account all the accomplishments requisite to a painter, no one made such near approaches to Da Vinci as did Luini; he having painted a vast number of heads which, in design, colouring, and composition, bear so strong a resemblance to those of the great luminary of this school, that out of Milan many of his pictures pass for Da Vinci's.

We must, however, observe here of Luini, as

we did just now of Cesare da Sesto; that he, too, in certain of his works approximates very closely to the style of Raphael. Whence, I suspect, has arisen the opinion entertained by some, that he had visited Rome; a circumstance which Bianconi with good reason calls in question; inclining rather to maintain the negative of that opinion. Leonardo's taste was so nearly allied to Raphael's, in the delicate, the graceful, and the accurate expression of the passions, that had not his attention been distracted by the multiplicity of his pursuits, and had he dispensed with something of his exquisite finish in order to arrive at greater facility of execution, greater elegance and fulness of contour; his style would almost spontaneously have coincided with that of Raphael, with which, more especially in some of the heads, it has great affinity. The same, I suspect, was the case with Luini, who had made Da Vinci's style his own, and who lived in an age that was now making rapid strides towards a freer and softer manner. Thus Luini began by painting in a style less full and bordering on the dry, as is sufficiently evident from his Pietà, at the church della Passione; but this style he subsequently went on moderating by degrees.

It is my opinion, that Luini was indebted for this style not so much to Rome, (from whence he may perhaps have had some few engravings and copies of the works of the artists who flourished there; as to the school of Da Vinci, with whose maxims I find him singularly imbued; but more especially did he owe it to his own genius, which, in its kind, was of the highest order, and indeed almost unrivalled. I say in its kind,—the soft, the attractive, the tender, the affecting. In those historical pieces relative to the Virgin, at Saronno, though the features are not actually the same, yet they bear a close resemblance, in point of beauty, dignity, and modesty, to those with which Raphael has invested her. They invariably appear in keeping with the story; whether that story represent the Virgin being led to the altar; or listening with wonder to the prophetic voice of Simeon; or, rapt in contemplation of the awful mystery, receiving the Wise Men of the East; or, betwixt grief and joy, interrogating the Child Jesus in the Temple, and saying, "Son, wherefore hast thou thus dealt with us?" In like manner, the other figures are invested with a sort of beauty adapted to their character—heads that seem as though they were alive—expressive looks and gestures that appear as if actually asking for an answer; combined, too, with a fertility of fancy, both in the drapery and the development of the passions, which is nevertheless strictly in conformity with truth,—a style in which every thing appears natural and spontaneous; while

rivets the eye at the first glance, engages it to examine the component parts, and makes it difficult to give over looking—such is Luini's style in the above-mentioned Temple.

GAUDENZIO FERRARI.

According to Lomazzo, Ferrari's principal master was Scotto, though he was subsequently under the care of Luini; while, at Vercelli, the story goes that he was first of all a pupil of Giovenone's. Novara, it is thought, possesses one of his earliest works,—an altar-piece at the cathedral, divided into various compartments, like those of the fifteenth century, and with the gildings so much applauded during that century. Vercelli has, in the church of St. Mark, a copy of the cartoon of S. Anna, to which are added St. Joseph and some other Saint,—a youthful effort like the other, and one which proves that Gaudenzio had betimes turned his eyes towards Leonardo; from whom, according to Vasari, he derived great advantage. While still a young man he went to Rome, where it is said he became one of Raphael's coadjutors; and from whence he brought back with him a style more elevated in design and more attracting in colouring than any thing to be found among the Milanese. Lomazzo (whose verdict Scanelli condemns) eulogizes him as one of the greatest painters the world has ever seen,—unjustly omitting Correggio. For, whoever compares the cupola of S. Giovanni at Parma with that of S. Maria near Saronno, painted by Gaudenzio about the same time, will find in the former a degree of beauty and perfection not to be met with in the latter. Indeed, though this latter abounds with figures whose beauty, variety, and attitudes we cannot but commend, it nevertheless exhibits, like certain other of Gaudenzio's works, some vestiges of the old style;—a dryness of manner, for example; a too stiff and symmetrical arrangement of the figures; Angels whose drapery is sometimes in the style of Mantegna; and here and there a figure executed, for the sake of relief, in stucco, and then coloured—a plan which he pursued elsewhere in the trappings of horses and other accessories, after the manner of Montorfano.

With the exception of these defects, which he wholly avoided in his more matured works, Gaudenzio is a painter of very distinguished merit; and, among the coadjutors of Raphael, is the one that makes the nearest approach to Perino and Giulio Romano. He, too, displays a most portentous fertility of fancy, though differing in kind from that of Giulio: the latter having employed himself principally on profane and lascivious subjects, while Gaudenzio devoted himself to those of a religious character; seeming to be endowed with a faculty almost unique, of expressing the majesty of the Divine Being, the mysteries of religion, the outward marks of devotion. His *forte* lay in the development of strong character; for though he was not apt to display much prominence of muscle, he was, to use Vasari's words, fond of singular attitudes—attitudes of a fierce and terrific character, wherever the subject required them. Such was his picture of Christ's Passion, in the Grazie, at Milan, where he had Titian for his competitor; and the Conversion of St. Paul, in the possession of the Conventuals at Vercelli; a work more like that of M. Angelo in the Pauline Chapel than any I have ever seen. In his other works also he delights in difficult foreshortenings, and introduces them continually. If he does not equal Raphael in grace and beauty, he still displays the same character in no small degree, as in the church of St. Christopher at Vercelli; where, besides the picture of St. Christopher himself, he has depicted on the walls various pieces relative to our Saviour, and certain others relative to Mary Magdalene.

To come now to other peculiarities observable in his style: Ferrari, contrary to the usual practice of the Milanese, displays such vivacity and sprightliness of colouring, that, in some of the churches where he has painted, there is no need to ask for his pictures; they invite and rivet the eye of the spectator at once, by flesh colours that are true to nature, and as diversified as their subjects, and drapery full of fancy and novelty, and exhibiting all the variety to be found in the different kinds of cloth. Still better, however, if we may be allowed to say so, did he succeed in depicting the mind than the body. This is one of the departments of art to which he paid most attention: in the works of few others do we meet with more eloquent gestures or more expressive heads. And, if at any time he embellishes his historical pieces with landscape or architecture, the landscape is accompanied, for the most part, by views of fantastic rocks, that delight us by their very novelty; while the architectural decorations are executed with a scrupulous attention to the truth of the perspective. This great man was either very little known by Vasari, or held in very little estimation by him; whence foreigners, who are apt to measure a man's merit by the figure he makes in history, are but little acquainted with him, and in their writings have almost wholly passed him over in silence.*

* Lomazzo, of whom Lanzi gives some account under this epoch, is more known by his works on painting than by his pictures.

MILANESE SCHOOL.

EPOCH III.

THE PROCACCINI AND OTHER PAINTERS, AS WELL OF OTHER STATES AS OF MILAN, ESTABLISH THERE A NEW ACADEMY AND NEW STYLES.

THE best among the followers of Da Vinci and Ferrari adopted, more or less, the new styles which, to the prejudice of the old, from time to time found their way into Milan. As early as Gaudenzio's time, Titian's Crown of Thorns had been received with much applause at Milan; whence some of his scholars went and established themselves there, and these were followed by artists from other places. To this we may add the misfortunes which befell the state, especially the plague, which afflicted it more than once during the same century; by which the native artists being carried off, strangers entered upon the tasks in which they had been engaged, as they would upon an inheritance void by the death of the original heir. The princely disposition of certain noble families, especially the Borromean family, contributed not a little to attract strangers. Many were the edi-

been erected or repaired by order of Charles and Frederick Borromeo; many were the edifices both in the city and elsewhere, that were by their means decorated with paintings; insomuch that it might with truth be said, that Milan was no less indebted to the Borromean princes, than was Florence to her Medici, or Mantua to her Gonzaghi. Not content with employing on the public works the ablest architects, sculptors, and painters that were to be met with, Frederick Borromeo raised together the few surviving embers, as it were, of Da Vinci's Academy, and, by vigorous efforts and at great expense, enriched the city with a new academy of the fine arts. Hence, the Milanese artists having been previously reduced to a small number, and the demand for painters to decorate the churches and other public edifices which were now springing up having increased, other styles were introduced into Milan by strangers, such as the Campi, the Semini, the Procaccini, the Nuvoloni, &c. To these nearly all the young artists of Milan and its dependencies were indebted for instruction; these men, beginning their career in that city about 1570, and continuing to work there even till after the year 1600, surpassed the old schools not so much by the excellence of their teaching, as by the allurements of their novelty; and at length by degrees extinguished them.

The Campi were among the most celebrated in

bring themselves into notice at Milan, and executed a great many works there; Bernardino more than any of the others. Subsequently the two Semini of Genoa made their appearance at Milan; where they also produced a considerable number of paintings, both of them imitating the Roman style more than that of any other school. But those who at that time both painted most themselves, and reared the greatest number of pupils at Milan, were the Procaccini of Bologna.

Ercole Procaccini is the head of this family. At Milan there still exist a good many works of his, by which we may be enabled to decide for ourselves whether most credit is due to Malvasia and Baldinucci, who describe him as "a painter of moderate talents;" or to Lomazzo, who styles him "a most happy imitator of the great Coreggio's colouring and gracefulness." To say the truth, as far as my judgment goes, he betrays, in some degree, a littleness of design, and, after the manner of the Florentines, a feebleness of colouring; a defect so common with the artists of that period, that I see not how it can be charged upon him alone. For the rest, he evinces a gracefulness, accuracy, and exactness, to be found in few of his contemporaries; nor is it improbable that this excessive diligence of his, in a city where the expeditious Fontana bore undisputed sway, may have been an obstacle in his way. But this quality, besides causing him to steer clear of mannerism, to which the age was but too prone, tended also to make him an excellent master; whose chief task consists in curbing the impatience and impetuosity of youth, and habituating them to precision and delicacy of finish. Hence from his school there proceeded several eminent painters, a Samacchini, a Sabbatini, a Bertoia. He also initiated in the art his three sons, Camillo, Giulio Cesare, and Carlo Antonio, the father of Ercole Procaccini the younger, each of whom formed pupils among the Milanese youth.

Camillo Procaccini is the only one of the three brothers who was known to Lomazzo, by whom he is described as one eminently skilled in design and colouring. He imbibed the first rudiments of art from his father, of whom he often reminds us in his heads and the distribution of his colours. He afterwards inspected the productions of other schools; and, if we are to credit certain biographers, exercised himself at Rome in copying the works of M. Angelo and Raphael; but, for his heads, he more especially studied Parmigianino, of whom we may discover marks of imitation in every one of his works. He was endowed with extraordinary facility both of invention and execution: his works, too, display an air of nature, a grace, a spirit, that fails not to please the eye, although it does not always satisfy the judgment. Nor is this to be wondered at; he having from the very first freed himself from the restraint imposed by his father's system of education, and executed works enough for any five painters, at Bologna, Ravenna, Reggio, Piacenza, Pavia, and Genoa; whence he was by many denominated the Vasari and the Zuccaro of Lombardy; though, to say the truth, he surpasses them in correctness of style and beauty of colouring. Milan, however, was the chief scene of his labours; and that city possesses many of his best works, with which he there brought himself into repute, as well as many of his worst, with which he gratified those who were taken with his fame.

Giulio Cesare Procaccini, the most celebrated of the Procaccini, after having for some time cultivated sculpture, and not without considerable success, turned his attention to painting, as the more respectable and less laborious pursuit. At Bologna he attended the school of the Caracci; and it is said that, having been offended by some cutting observation of Annibale's, he struck him a severe blow. Giulio's time, however, was more especially devoted to the study of Correggio's works, and, in the opinion of many, no one succeeded better in imitating his noble style. In cabinet pictures and those that contain few figures, where such imitation is a matter of less difficulty, he has often been confounded with Coreggio himself; although the gracefulness of Giulio's style is not so natural and easy as that of his model, nor the laying on of his colours so strong and vigorous. He left behind him a great number of historical pieces, as the Passage of the Red Sea, at S. Vittore, at Milan, and still more at Genoa, which have been noticed by Soprani; and what, considering their number, is matter of surprise, he displays exactness of design, fertility of fancy, together with considerable skill in anatomy and in the disposition of the drapery; taking care to accompany the whole with an elevation of manner, which, unless I am much mistaken, he derived from the Carracci.

Carlantonio Procaccini. To these two we must add Carlantonio Procaccini, not as an historical, but as a landscape painter, and one who was in considerable repute for the representation of fruits and flowers. Of these he painted a great many for the different collections at Milan; and these having been approved of at the court, which at that time was Spanish, he received a great many orders for Spain; whence, though he was the worst painter of the family, he became the most known.

The Procaccini opened a school at Milan, and had the reputation of being kind and attentive masters, insomuch that they reared in that city and the surrounding territory such a multitude of pupils, that it would be hopeless as well as useless to attempt to give an account of them all.

The last among the strangers who taught at Milan was *Panfilo Nuvolone*, of Cremona, one who was more remarkable for diligence than fertility of fancy. In his altar-pieces, as well as other historical works which he painted for the Ducal gallery at Parma, he aimed rather at perfecting his figures than at multiplying their number.

Daniele Crespi is one of those illustrious Italians who are scarcely known beyond the limits of their native place. He was a man of rare genius, who, having been placed first under the care of Cerano, next under that of Giulio Cesare Procaccini, beyond all doubt surpassed the former, and, as many will have it, the latter also; though he died before he had completed his fortieth year. Endowed with great quickness of penetration and facility of execution, he had the tact to imitate what was best and avoid what was less commendable in his master's style. It is probable, too, that having made himself acquainted with the maxims of the Carracci, though without attending their school, he adopted and practised them with success. So far as regards the distribution of the colours, he imitates them closely; he displays variety, but at the same time, choice, in the style of his heads; taking care to suit the attitude to the emotion intended to be expressed; succeeding more especially in investing the heads of his Saints with an air of virtue and devotion. In the grouping of his figures he adopts a plan so natural, and yet so judicious, that not one of them could well change its place: the drapery is well diversified, and in the figures of the opulent, very costly. His colouring, both in his oil-paintings and frescos, is remarkable for its vigour. He is one of those rare painters who are continually vieing with themselves; doing his utmost that each succeeding work may surpass his previous efforts. The defects discoverable in his earlier works, are corrected in his later performances; and the great qualities which in the former seem to be just developing themselves, in the latter appear matured and brought to perfection."

* The true names of the persons [illegible] under this head are Bernardino [illegible], denominated, from the name of the place where he was born, [illegible] and [illegible] Campi, who, [illegible] [illegible] [illegible] Campi. [illegible] [illegible] [illegible] [illegible] [illegible] [illegible] [illegible] [illegible] [illegible] [illegible]

BOLOGNESE SCHOOL.

EPOCH I.

THE OLD MASTERS.

We have already observed, in the course of this work, that pre-eminence in painting, no less than pre-eminence in letters and arms, has successively fallen to the lot of different states; and wherever the art has fixed its seat, some branch of it, that was less understood or less attended to by preceding painters, has been brought to perfection. Towards the close of the sixteenth century, there was no longer any species of beauty, or any aspect under which it could appear, to which some great master had not addressed himself, and of which he had not given a representation; so that the artist, whether he liked or not, while he sought to imitate nature, was constrained at the same time to imitate the best masters; the formation of a new style consisting thenceforth only in a skilful adaptation of the older methods. Thus imitation was now become the sole means of attaining to distinction; as it appeared impossible to design figures in a more masterly manner than Bonarrotti or Da Vinci, to invest them with more grace than Raphael, to colour them more to the life than Titian, to impart to them more fire and animation than Tintoretto, to set them off with richer decoration than Paul Veronese, or to present them to the eye at every degree of distance, and under every aspect, with greater skill and roundness, and a more enchanting effect, than had already been done by Correggio. Accordingly, the path of imitation was at that time pursued by every school; though, to say the truth, with very little judgment. Every school saw in a manner the eyes of its founder; and had no idea of distinguishing itself in any department but that in which he had surpassed all others. With these servile imitators, distinction, even in this respect, consisted in nothing more than constantly copying the same figures, and executing them in a more hasty and capricious manner, or, at least, introducing them on improper occasions. In every one of their pictures, the followers of Raphael carried the ideal style to excess; the followers of Michael Angelo, the anatomical; while needless fire, vivacity and unnecessary foreshortenings reappeared in every historical piece of the Venetian and Lombard painters, even where the subject was of the quietest kind.

There were, as we have already had occasion to observe, in every school, some few who rose above the prejudices of the times, and, so to speak, lifted their heads above the mists that then obscured Italy; studying the masters of different states for the purpose of uniting what was best in each: above all, the Campi of Cremona set a commendable example in this respect. But these artists, unequal in acquirements and talent, divided into different schools, directed by private interests, accustomed to guide their pupils only in the same path they pursued themselves, and, moreover, always confined within the limits of their native province, afforded no instruction to the rest of Italy, or at least did not disseminate the method of a correct and judicious style of imitation. This was an honour reserved for Bologna, whose destiny was said to be teaching, as governing was said to be the destiny of Rome; and it was the work, not of an academy, but of a single family. The Caracci, rich in genius, united in their efforts, and eager in their pursuit of the secrets rather than the profits of painting, hit upon the true method of imitation; disseminating it at first over the neighbouring Romagna, and thence communicating it to the rest of Italy, where, in the course of a short time, it spread from sea to sea. The great principle they inculcated was, that the painter should divide his attention between nature and art, keeping each of them in view in its turn; and that, according to his natural talent and peculiar disposition, he should select what was most commendable in both. Thus the Bolognese school, which was the last in rising to eminence, became the first in the art of teaching, and, after having been the pupil of all, proceeded to give lessons to all; producing, in the sequel, a number of styles, (that may in some sort be called original,) as great as was the number of the Carracci and their scholars.

Franco Bolognese. Oderigi d' Agubbio, celebrated for his illuminations,* I may refer to the school of Bologna, probably as a pupil, certainly as a master; and, according to Vellutello, as the master of Franco Bolognese. Franco is the first of the Bolognese artists who formed any considerable number of pupils; and is, as it were, the Giotto of this school. He is, however, not a little inferior to the Florentine Giotto, so far as we can judge from the few remaining works of his to be seen in the Malvezzi collection. The best authenticated piece is a figure of the Virgin seated on a throne, and bearing the date 1313,—a work that

* Oh! dissi lui, non se' tu Oderisi,
L'onor d' Agubbio, e l'onor di quell' arte
Che alluminar è chiamata a Parisi?
Frate, diss' egli, più ridon le carte
Che pennelleggia Franco Bolognese;
L'onor è tutto or suo, e mio in parte.
DANTE.

may be compared to the performances of Cimabue and Guido da Siena. To him also are ascribed two very pretty little pictures and other illuminations of the like kind.

The best of Franco's scholars were, according to Malvasia, Vitale da Bologna, Lorenzo, Simone dei Crocifissi, Jacopo Avanzi, and a certain Cristoforo; the fresco paintings of which artists are still to be seen at the Madonna di Mezzaratta. This church is with respect to the Bolognese school what the Campo Santo of Pisa is with regard to the Florentine,—an arena where the best artists of the thirteenth century, who flourished in those parts, wrought in competition with each other. They have not the simplicity, the elegance, the grouping, which constitute the merit of the Giotteschi; but they evince a degree of fancy, a fire, a method of colouring, which Buonarroti and the Caracci, considering the time at which they lived, thought by no means contemptible: in that century, when these pictures began to exhibit symptoms of decay, they advised and promoted their restoration. Hence, in the above-mentioned church, there were painted at various times historical pieces from the Old and New Testament, not only by the aforesaid scholars of Franco, but by Galasso of Ferrara, and an unknown imitator of Giotto's style, whom Lamo in his manuscript maintains to be Giotto himself.

Lippo di Dalmasio.—From Vitale's school proceeded Lippo di Dalmasio, denominated Lippo dalle Madonne. His style differs not from that of most of the old masters, except perhaps in the better blending of the colours, and the better disposition of the drapery; to which, however, he adds very deep gilt borders, as was every where the fashion about the beginning of the fourteenth century. His heads are of a beautiful and peculiar character, especially in certain of his Madonnas, which Guido Reni was never tired of contemplating; being accustomed to say, that Lippo was possessed of an almost supernatural faculty of combining in the same countenance, the majesty, the sanctity, and sweetness of disposition that became the Mother of the Incarnate Word; and that in this respect no modern had ever equalled him.

Marco Zoppo.—Subsequent to the year 1410, the date of the last of Lippo's performances, the Bolognese school somewhat declined. Not, however, but that there were still, as far as the times would permit, some tolerable painters in Bologna and throughout Romagna. But the one who forms an epoch in the school, is Marco Zoppo, who, having studied under Lippo, subsequently placed himself under the care of Squarcione. He also visited Venice, where he remained some time, and where he painted for the Observanti of Pesaro a picture representing the Virgin seated on a throne, and accompanied by John the Baptist, St. Francis, and other Saints; adding this inscription, "Marco Zoppo da Bologna dip: in Venexia 1471." This is the largest of his works that has come down to us: and from this and some few other pieces to be found in that church, and at Bologna, we may form an idea of his style. Their composition is the same as prevails in the works of the artists of the fourteenth century, (especially the Venetians,) which he probably introduced into Bologna; where it lasted till the time of Francia and his school, with scarcely any variation; save that now and then an Angel was represented on the steps of the throne, sometimes with a lyre, sometimes without. This style has not the light elegance observable in Mantegna's; on the contrary, it inclines rather to the homely, especially in the drawing of the feet: it is, however, less mechanical and more easy in the folds of the drapery: and perhaps more harmonious in the choice of the colours. The parts of the body exposed to view are as studiously designed as in the works of Crivelli, or any other painter of that age; and the figures themselves, as well as the accessories, are executed with the utmost care.

Francesco Francia distinguished himself greatly in that style which is denominated the modern antique; as is observable in very many collections, where his Madonnas are placed beside those of Pietro Perugino and Gian Bellini. His manner holds, as it were, a middle course between that of those two masters, partaking of them both. In choice, and the character of the colouring, it approaches Pietro's style; while in the fulness of the contours, and the dexterous management and ample folds of the drapery, it is more nearly allied to that of Bellini. In the heads it does not come up to the sweetness and gracefulness observable in those of the former; but it is more dignified, as well as more diversified, than that of the latter. It emulates them both in the accessories of landscape; though, in this respect, and in splendour of architectural ornaments, it falls short of them. In the composition of a picture, it delights to place the Infant Saviour, not so much in the lap of the Virgin, as in another place,—a practice of ancient date in that school—adding now and then, a half-length figure of some Saint, after the manner of the Venetians of that period. Upon the whole, however, it approaches nearer to the Roman school; and the fact recorded by Malvasia—that his Madonnas are by the uninitiated ascribed to Pietro Perugino—is by no means of rare occurrence. At Bologna there were also some of his frescoes, of which Vasari speaks with commendation; and there, as well as elsewhere, many altar-pieces of his still exist, containing figures of a larger scale than those usually found in Bellini's and Perugino's works,—a peculiarity which was long a distinguishing merit of the Bolognese school.

Antonio da Forli, commonly called Melozzo.—Doubts have arisen in my mind as to whether Squarcione really was the master of Melozzo, a name held in high veneration by the profession, for having been the first to set the example of foreshortening on ceilings; an art known by the name of *di sotto in su*, and the most difficult and rigorous within the whole compass of painting. In perspective, after the time of Paolo Uccello, considerable progress had been made by means of Piero della Francesca, a celebrated geometrician, and by certain Lombard painters; but the art of painting ceilings with the delightful illusion afterwards introduced was an honour reserved for Melozzo. His style, all things considered, approaches nearer to that of Mantegna and the Paduan school than to that of any other: the heads, in point of shape, colouring, and movement, have considerable beauty, and are nearly all of them foreshortened: due care is evinced in the gradation of the lights, and the proper introduction of the shadows, so that the figures may be well rounded, and, as it were, appear endowed with motion: there is also an air of dignity and grandeur in the principal figure and the white robe that envelops it: together with a delicacy of pencilling, a finish, and gracefulness in every part.*

BOLOGNESE SCHOOL.

EPOCH II.

ITS DIFFERENT STYLES, FROM THE TIME OF FRANCIA DOWN TO THAT OF THE CARRACCI.

WHILE, after the discovery of the modern style, the other schools of Italy were proceeding to cultivate it, by following each of them some leader of its own, the Bolognese painters, not having any one from whom they could learn it in their native place, either betook themselves to other places, for the purpose of acquainting themselves with it under the actual instruction of living masters; or, if they remained at home, strove to acquire it from such strangers as had either wrought there, or, at least, sent thither specimens of their works.*

* The more distinguished of those omitted under this epoch are—Lorenzo Costa, the two Aspertini, Chiodarolo, Niccolò Rondinelli, the two Cotignola, and Palmegiani.

† Besides the St. Cecilia of Raphael, Bologna could then boast Giulio Romano's St. John and Garofalo's Zacharias. Parmigianino had left behind him his St. Roch and his St. Margaret, which

Bagnacavallo.—The first to introduce the modern style at Bologna, were—Bartolommeo Ramenghi, (from the name of his native place, denominated Bagnacavallo,) and Innocenzio Francucci da Imola. Bagnacavallo had wrought at Rome under Raphael, and certainly not without advantage. He had not Giulio's or Perino's depth of design, but in his style of colouring he approached, and perhaps equalled them; while, in the gracefulness of his heads, those at least of an infantine character, he surpassed them. In the composition of his pictures he took Raphael for his model; as is evident from the celebrated Dispute of St. Augustine at the Scopetini, where we recognize the principles observable in the school of Athens, and in other copious and celebrated works of Raphael's. Indeed, Bagnacavallo, in the subjects which he handled, not unfrequently contented himself with merely copying Raphael, affirming that it was madness to attempt to do better.

Innocenzio, a native of Imola, resided almost constantly at Bologna, and entered Francia's school in the year 1506; though we must not from thence infer with Malvasia, that he did not spend some

rank among his happiest performances. Girolamo da Carpi, Niccolò Abati, Girolamo da Trevigi, and Tommaso Laureti, had also made some stay at Bologna. And the same may be said of Boldraffio, a scholar of Da Vinci's, as well as of M. Angelo himself, and his imitator Vasari.

years at Florence in company with Albertinelli. Vasari asserts that he did, and his style, which resembles that of the more ancient Florentines of the period in question, corroborates the assertion. He executed a good many altar-pieces, composing them in the manner of those of the fourteenth century; but, after the example of Fra Bartolommeo and Andrea del Sarto, placing the Virgin aloft divested of the gilt borders and glories in vogue among the old masters, and grouping and disposing the accompanying Saints with admirable skill; displaying, too, some degree of novelty in the way in which he distributed the attendant angels, which were ranged upon the steps and poised in the air. Into his altar-pieces he sometimes used to introduce small historical subjects, as in that at S. Giacomo di Bologna, where at the foot of the picture he painted a Cratch, very much in the style of Raphael. This, indeed, was the style to which he always aspired, and to which he made nearer approaches than very many even of Raphael's scholars themselves. In point of keeping, majesty, and correctness, he is considered superior to Francia and Bagnacavallo. I am not aware that he ever produced works of any great novelty, or possessing much fire and animation; nor, indeed, could such works be much adapted to the nature of his genius, which all accounts describe as of a quiet and placid character.

Primaticcio.—The fame of the two masters above recorded did not at that time reach far beyond the limits of their native place, being eclipsed by that of many other contemporaries, who were then looked upon as the great luminaries of art; among these was Giulio Romano. The repute in which Giulio was held, attracted to Mantua Francesco Primaticcio, who had been initiated in design by Innocenzio, in colouring by Bagnacavallo. Under Giulio Romano he acquired a taste for large historical pieces and compositions on a grand scale, as well as for those decorations in metal and stucco fitted only for a palace. Thus, having studied for six years at Mantua, he was sent by Giulio into France, to Francis I.; and though Rosso of Florence had already arrived there a year before him, and produced various works there, nevertheless, according to Vasari, "the first stuccoes, as well as the first frescoes of any consequence, that were executed in France, took their rise from Primaticcio." His performances in that country are described by Felibien; who says of him in a strain of panegyric, that, "the French painters are indebted to Primaticcio and M. Nicolo (dell' Abate) for many beautiful works, and we may fairly say that they were the first to introduce into France the Roman style, and an idea of the beauties of the painting and sculpture of the ancients."

TIBALDI.—Pellegrino Pellegrini, from his father's name denominated Tibaldi, seems to have been born under the same star as Primaticcio and Nicolò: he was a native of Valsolda in the Milanese; but passed his childhood and youth at Bologna. He did at the court of Spain what the two preceding artists did at that of France; he embellished that court with paintings, as well as contributed to improve its taste in architecture: there, too, he formed pupils, and from thence he brought back wealth enough to enable him to purchase the Marquisate of Valsolda, where his father and his uncle, previous to their going to Bologna, had lived in poverty as common masons. It is not known from whom this great man derived the first rudiments of art. Vasari will have it, that he was indebted for them to the paintings in the refectory of S. Michele in Bosco, which, while still a youth, Tibaldi copied, together with other choice works at Bologna. After that, he makes him arrive in Rome in the year 1547, for the purpose of studying the best works to be found there; and, after a residence of three years in that city, makes him return to Bologna, still a young man but a proficient in art. His style was in great measure formed after the model of M. Angelo, exhibiting the same grandeur, the same skill in anatomy, the same vigour, and the same felicity of foreshortening; but, at the same time, attenpered with such a degree of softness, that the Carracci used to call him *Michael Angelo reformed*. In the Institute at Bologna is the first work that he executed there after the year 1550, the best, in the judgment of Vasari, that he ever produced. It consists chiefly of subjects taken from the Odyssey. But whatever commendation Vasari may have bestowed on this work, the Carracci, whose opinion ought to have greater weight, have led us to think still more highly of Tibaldi's paintings at S. Jacopo,—paintings which both they and their scholars studied with the greatest assiduity.

Fontana.—While the three great masters already mentioned continued to reside, the two first in France, the third at Milan and subsequently in Spain; the art, instead of advancing, rather retrograded at Bologna. Fontana, whose long life took in the whole period of which we are treating, and even extended beyond it, was born during the life-time of Francia. Educated by Imola, who at his death made choice of him to finish one of his altar-pieces; becoming afterwards, and for a considerable time, the assistant of Vaga and Vasari; he continued constantly employed, either executing works of his own or instructing his scholars, till the Carracci, who had at one time been his disciples, stripped him both of orders and of followers. For this he was indebted to nobody but himself. Devoted to pleasure (the deadliest fice to the reputation of an artist,) he had no means of indulging his fondness for it but by undertaking more than he could do, and executing his paintings in a slovenly manner. He was blessed with a fertility of fancy, a boldness of temper, and an extent of information, well calculated to fit him for works on a large scale. Hence renouncing Francucci's careful finishings, he adopted Vasari's method, and, like him, painted a great many works in a very short space of time, and nearly all of them in the same style. His design betrays greater negligence than Vasari's, his attitudes have more fire and animation, while his colours present the more yellowish and unbroken appearance; though they evince a somewhat greater degree of delicacy. His chief merit lay in portrait painting, and the portraits of his to be seen in different collections are even now more prized than are his historical pieces in the different churches. It was in consequence of this talent, that Bonarroti presented him to Julius III., by whom he was rewarded with a pension. He was also employed by the three Pontiffs who succeeded next after Julius, and was looked upon as the best portrait painter of his time.

Lorenzo Sabbatini, styled also Lorenzino of Bologna, was one of the most graceful and finished painters of his day. In the different collections, I have sometimes heard him ranked, by the knowing, among the scholars of Raphael; led into this error by his Holy Families, of which the design and composition are in the best style of the Roman school; although the colouring is invariably more feeble. I have, however, seen figures of the Virgin, as well as Angels, of his, in cabinet pictures, that might pass for the work of Parmigianino: and the same manner he adopted in his altar-pieces. He was also distinguished as a fresco painter; displaying correctness of design, fertility of invention, universality of subject, and, what is more surprising, extraordinary rapidity of execution. In consequence of these merits, he was not only employed by many noble families at Bologna, but on going to Rome, as Baglione will have it, during the pontificate of Gregory XIII., he was held in great repute in that city: even his naked figures were highly applauded; though while at Bologna, he had paid but little attention to this branch of art. In the Pauline Chapel he represented some passages of the life of St. Paul; in the Sala Regia, Faith triumphing over Infidelity; in the *Galleria* and the *Loggie*, various other subjects, always in competition with the best masters, and always with applause. Thus amidst the multitude of artists who at that time flocked to Rome from every quarter, he was selected to preside over the decorations of the Vatican; in which employ he died in 1577, in the vigour of his age.

Orazio Samachini, the contemporary and intimate friend of Sabbatini, and one who survived him but a short time, began by imitating Pellegrino and the Lombard masters. Repairing afterwards to Rome, and getting employed on the paintings of the Sala Regia, he distinguished himself in the Roman style, and gained the applause of Vasari, as well as afterwards of Borghini and Lomazzo. In this new style, however, he satisfied every one else better than himself, and on his return to Bologna used to regret that he had ever quitted Upper Italy, where he might have carried to perfection the method he first pursued, without seeking for one more modern. He had, however, good reason to be satisfied with the one that he adopted; made up as it was of so many different styles, and so modified by his own genius, that it exhibits in every feature much of the novel and singular. The Purification at S. Jacopo is an exquisite performance; where the principal figures enchant us by an expression of piety at once tender and elevated; while the children who stand prattling beside the altar, and the damsel who is seen holding the two doves in a little basket, and watching them so narrowly, ravish us by their simplicity and grace. The only fault connoisseurs have been able to find with it, is the excessive diligence it betrays; the execution and completion of this work having occupied him for several years.

He is thought to have evinced most aptitude for copious frescos, on which he imprinted, as it were, the stamp of a genius at once comprehensive, ardent, and expeditious, without giving way to those subsequent alterations and corrections, with which, as we have seen, he used to torture his oil paintings.

Bartolommeo Passerotti was endowed with an extraordinary talent for designing with the pen, a talent which attracted Agostino Carracci to his school, and which served as a guide to the latter in the art of engraving. He also composed a book, of which the subject was to teach so much of the structure and anatomy of the human frame as might be requisite for a painter; and he it was who, to display his knowledge in this respect, set the example at Bologna of giving variety to altar-pieces by the introduction of naked *torsos*. Among these the best were—the Beheading of St. Paul at the Three Fountains in Rome—and the Virgin accompanied by various Saints, in the church of S. Giacomo at Bologna; a work painted in competition with the Carracci, and honoured with their applause. A Tizio of his was also celebrated, and when exhibited to the public, was, by the Bolognese artists, taken for a work of M. Angelo's. It was not often that he took such exquisite pains; he kept, for the most part, to the easy and the free, somewhat resembling Cesari, though more correct. In portrait painting, however, he is above

the autumn sun. In this department of art Guido ranked him among the greatest painters after Titian, not considering him to have been inferior to the Caracci themselves; to whom, indeed, Passerotti's portraits in different collections are sometimes assigned.

Dionysius Calvart, a native of Antwerp, repaired to Bologna in early youth, with some reputation for landscape; and with a view to historical painting attended first Fontana's school, and next that of Sabbatini, to whom he was of considerable use in the decorations of the Vatican. Quitting him also, and employing himself for a very short period in designing Raphael's pictures, he returned to Bologna, opened a studio there, and educated no less than a hundred and thirty-seven scholars, some of whom turned out admirable painters. Calvart himself was an eminent painter for that age; well versed in perspective, which he had acquired from Fontana, and correct and graceful in design, after the manner of Sabbatini. He was also a good colourist in the Flemish style; a quality for which the Bolognese looked upon him as one of the restorers of their school, which in this branch of the art was then on the decline. If there was any thing of mannerism in his style, any thing unbecoming or exaggerated in the action of his figures; the one is imputable to the age in which he lived, the other to his own temper, which all accounts describe as in the highest degree turbulent and fiery. The different galleries abound with little pictures of his on subjects from the New Testament, painted for the most part on copper; they charm us by the multitude of the figures, and the richness of the colouring. Orders for pictures of this kind were then very frequent at Bologna; and were commonly given by newly professed nuns, who used to take such little pictures with them to their convent, for the purpose of decorating their cells. Calvart used to make his scholars take copies of these, and then retouching them himself, met with a very ready sale for them in Italy and Flanders. Those copied for him by Albani and Guido, who were at one time his scholars, are the most pleasing of all; and are distinguishable by their superior purity as well as by a somewhat greater boldness and facility of touch. Among the most celebrated of his altar-pieces, are—the St. Michael in the church of S. Petronio—and the Purgatory alle Grazie; from which, and certain others, the best of the Caracci would acknowledge they derived considerable advantage.

Bartolommeo Cesi must also be ranked among those eminent masters who paved the way for the improved style of the Caracci. From him Tiarini acquired the art of fresco-painting, and from his works it was that Guido first caught the idea of striking out his own sweet and graceful style. On observing a picture of Cesi's, one is sometimes led to doubt whether it is not one of the earlier works of Guido. He evinces but little boldness of manner; copying every thing from nature, selecting the best forms at every period of life, and investing them but sparingly with ideal beauties; his drapery is somewhat scanty, his attitudes measured, his colouring graceful rather than strong. He was esteemed by the Carracci, and was a general favourite with the profession for the integrity of his character and the love he bore the art.*

BOLOGNESE SCHOOL.

EPOCH III.

THE CARRACCI AND THEIR PUPILS.

To write the history of the Carracci and their followers is almost the same thing as writing the history of Italian painting in general for the last two centuries. In the foregoing books we have taken a survey of almost every school; and in most of them, sooner or later, have found either the Car-

* Of the other painters of this epoch, the best were—Gio. Battista Cremonini, Cesare Baglione, and Luca Longhi.

ceeded themselves, or their scholars, or at least their successors, engaged in overthrowing the ancient maxims, and introducing new ones in their stead; insomuch that he who could not in some respect or other be called a follower of the Caracci, seemed scarcely to merit the name of painter. Now, as it is gratifying to the traveller, after having long followed the course of some noble river, to trace it upward to its source; so, I trust, it will not be unacceptable to the reader to be made acquainted with the principles from which this new style derived its origin, and owing to which it in a short time overran every other school. What to me seems most surprising in the matter is, that this style should have originated with Lodovico Caracci, a young man who, during his earlier years, appeared to be slow of understanding, and fitter to grind colours than to harmonize and apply them. Fontana, whose pupil he was at Bologna, and Tintoretto, under whom he studied at Venice, advised him, as one altogether unqualified for painting, to change his profession: his fellow-scholars, taunting him with this slowness of understanding, derisively applied to him the epithet of the Ox: every thing tended to dishearten him: he did not, however, suffer himself to be discouraged, and, so far from being dismayed by the difficulties he encountered, took them as a motive for increased exertion. His slowness, indeed, was the effect of deep penetration rather than of a confused understanding; he dreaded the ideal style as a rock on which so many of his contemporaries had made shipwreck; in every object nature was what he had in view; he exacted from himself a reason for every line he drew; considering it the duty of a youthful artist to aim invariably at excellence, till excellence becomes habitual, and thus paves the way for expedition.

Fixed in his purpose, therefore, as at Bologna he had studied the best masters among his fellow-countrymen, so at Venice he adopted Titian and Tintoretto as his models: from Venice he proceeded to Florence, and improved his taste by observing the pictures of Andrea, and listening to the instructions of Passignano. The Florentine school had then reached that crisis which we have already described in treating of its fourth epoch. Nothing could be more advantageous to the youthful Lodovico than to witness there the wranglings between the partisans of the old and the followers of the new styles; nor could he any where have met with a better opportunity than these bickerings afforded him, of penetrating into the causes of the decline of painting and the means of effecting its restoration. These circumstances, though hitherto but little noticed, were of no small assistance to him in his attempts to bring about a reformation and improvement in the art. The last of the Florentine artists, with a view to improve upon the languid colouring of their masters, had turned their attention to the works of Correggio and his followers; and their example, I suspect, induced Lodovico to leave Florence and repair to Parma, where, observes his biographer, he devoted all his time to the studying of the performances of that master and those of Parmigianino. On his return to Bologna, though well received and looked upon as an accomplished painter, he found nevertheless that a single individual, especially one so reserved and cautious as himself, could ill contend against an entire school; unless, doing as Cigoli had done at Florence, he could form a party amongst the rising generation at Bologna.

This he sought to form, in the first instance, among his own relatives. His brother Paolo cultivated painting, but was very deficient in judgment and ability, and fit for nothing else but to execute in a tolerable manner the designs of others: of him, therefore, Lodovico made little account; but he entertained great hopes of two of his cousins. He had a paternal uncle named Antonio, a tailor by trade, who brought up his two sons, Agostino and Annibale, at home; and such was the talent these two evinced for design, that Lodovico, when he was now advanced in years, used to say, that during the many years he had filled the office of a teacher, he had never had a single scholar to equal them. The former of these devoted himself to the goldsmith's art, which has ever been the school of the best engravers; the latter was at once the scholar and the assistant of his father in his calling. Though brothers, their dispositions and habits were so opposite, that they could not endure each other, and were little less than sworn foes. An accomplished scholar, Agostino was constantly to be seen in the company of the learned, nor was there any science on which he was not capable of conversing; at once a philosopher, a geometrician, and a poet; of polished manners, ready wit, and averse from the habits of the lower orders. Annibale, on the other hand, affected no learning beyond the mere ability to read and write; a certain innate churlishness inclined him to taciturnity; and whenever he was under the necessity of speaking, it was usually in a contemptuous, satirical, or quarrelsome tone.

At the school of Lodovico, their attention being turned to the art of painting, they betrayed even here the difference of their dispositions. Agostino was naturally hesitating and fastidious, slow to resolve, and hard to please, and never met with a difficulty which he did not fairly face and set himself to overcome: Annibale, who, like a multitude of others, was quick to execution, impatient of speculation and delay, sought every means to evade the difficulties of art, to pursue the easier path, and produce a great deal in a short time. Had they fallen into other hands, Agostino would have become another Samacchini, Annibale another Passerotti; nor would painting by their means have made a single step in advance. But their wary cousin, to whose care they were committed, saw that it would be necessary to imitate Isocrates, who, while superintending the education of Ephorus and Theopompus, was wont to say, that with the one he employed the spur, with the other the rein. With the like view Lodovico consigned Agostino to the care of Fontana, a master whose mode of execution was rapid and unconstrained; retaining Annibale in his own studio, where works were finished with greater delicacy. By these means, too, he managed to keep them apart, till time should, by degrees, extinguish the enmity subsisting between them, and convert it into friendship; when, devoted to the same pursuit, they should unite their capital, and each derive assistance from the other. In the course of a few years he found them sufficiently reconciled, and, in 1580, afforded them an opportunity of visiting Parma and Venice. During this visit, Agostino made considerable accessions to his various information, improved his designs; and as, before he set out from Bologna, he had acquired some skill in the art of engraving under Domenico Tibaldi, so, at Venice, he made such rapid progress in it under Cort, that the latter, out of mere jealousy, dismissed him from his studio; but in vain. Agostino was already looked upon as the Marc Antonio of his time. Annibale, now that he had but one occupation to attend to, turned all his thoughts, at Parma, and afterwards at Venice, to the art of painting; profiting both by the performances and the conversation of those illustrious men with whom at that time the Venetian school was thronged. It was then, or shortly afterwards, that he executed some most beautiful copies of Correggio's, Titian's, and Paolo's works; as well as some little pieces of his own in the same style. Of these I met with a few at Genoa, in the possession of the Marquis Durazzo, in different but very pleasing styles.

On their return to their native place, though now accomplished artists, they had for a long time to struggle against fortune. Their first works, representing certain portions of the story of Jason, on a frieze of the Casa Favi, although executed under the superintendence of Lodovico, were, by the older painters, treated with insufferable scorn, as deficient in accuracy and elegance. The repute in which these masters were held, men who had visited Rome, who were celebrated by poets, honoured with diplomas, and regarded by a degenerate age as the pillars of art, gave weight to their censures. Their disciples echoed their cry.

logy, and the multitude repeated them; and the endless animadversions of a populace, whose continual conversation is carried on with as much vivacity as a declamation or a dispute would be elsewhere, continually ringing in the ears of the Carracci, confounded and dismayed them. It is said, that Lodovico and Agostino were on the point of giving way to the current, and returning to the old style; but that Annibale dissuaded them from it, exhorting them to oppose works to words; or rather, to oppose to the works of the elder masters, feeble and mannered as they were, others that might have force and truth to recommend them. This advice was followed, and at length brought about the projected revolution; but in order to facilitate and accelerate it, it became necessary to win over to their party those youthful students who formed the hope of another and a more auspicious age. This the Carracci effected by opening an academy of painting, which they styled that of the *Incamminati*, furnishing it with casts, designs, and engravings, in as great abundance as those of their rivals; introducing into their plan a school for the study of the naked figure, as well as of perspective, anatomy, and every other requisite of the art; and conducting it with a judgment and kindliness of feeling, which could not fail, in a short time, to attract a crowd of pupils. Its success, too, may in some measure be attributed to the violent temper of Dionysius Calvart, who used to beat his pupils without mercy for the most trifling faults; insomuch that Guido, Albani, and Domenichino, betook themselves to the studio of the Carracci. Panico also left the school of Fontana in order to enter that of the Carracci; while the more promising youths flocked to it from all quarters, and gradually drew after them the common herd of students. At length every other academy was closed; every other school was transformed into a solitude; every other name gave place to the name of the Carracci; on them devolved the principal orders, to them was awarded the highest praise. Their humbled rivals now changed their tone; especially when the great saloon of the Magnani palace, that miracle of Carraccesque art, was thrown open to the admiring eyes of the public. It was then that Cesi declared himself a convert to the new style; it was then that Fontana lamented his advanced age precluded him from adopting it: Calvart alone, with his wonted arrogance, ventured to censure the work, and was the last to resign his competition, or at least to hold his tongue.

It is fit that we should here give some account of the system pursued, and the maxims held in a school, which, besides producing such illustrious pupils, contributed also to perfect their masters;

it being an indisputable truth, that teaching is the shortest road to learning. The three cousins were unanimous in their design of imparting instruction without cupidity and without envy; but the most laborious parts of this duty devolved upon Agostino. He had put forth a short treatise on perspective and architecture; and on this he gave lectures in the school. He explained to his scholars the nature of the bones and the muscles, designating them by their respective names; in this he was assisted by one Lanzoni, an anatomist, who also secretly supplied the students with bodies for the purpose of making the necessary dissections. Agostino took his subjects sometimes from history, sometimes from fable; explaining them, and making designs from them, which on certain days he exposed to view, and submitted to the opinion of competent judges, in order that they might decide on their respective merits; as appears from a note addressed to Cavi, one of those judges. By the fortunate candidates the glory of success was deemed a sufficient reward; poets assembled to sing their praises, while in the midst of them was seen Agostino celebrating with harp and voice the progress of his pupils. These latter were moreover instructed in the true principles of criticism: they were taught to observe the works of others, and mark whatever there was in them deserving of attention.

dation or censure: their own works, too, were exposed to view, and did not escape animadversion whenever they deserved it; indeed, whenever any one could not give a satisfactory reason for what he had done, he had to cancel it on the spot. Every one was at liberty to pursue his own favourite path: nay, every one was expressly directed to that particular style to which the bent of his inclination led him; and hence it is that so many different styles proceeded from the same studio: each of them, however, was required to have for its basis, reason, nature, and imitation. Whenever there occurred any serious doubt, recourse was had to Lodovico's opinion; the daily exercises in design were superintended by his two cousins, young men remarkable for industry and application, and sworn foes to sloth. Even the recreations of the students were made subservient to the advancement of art: to draw landscapes, or to compose some caricature, were the usual occupations of Annibale and his pupils whenever they sought relaxation from severer studies.

The maxim of the Carracci, of combining an accurate observation of nature with a judicious imitation of all the best masters, constituted the leading principle of their school; although, as we have observed, they contrived to modify it according to their different dispositions. Their object was to bring into one view whatever they had met with most deserving of commendation in every other school; and in this they pursued two different plans. In the first they followed the method of those poets, who in different Canzoni take different models for imitation; in one, for instance, borrowing from Petrarch, in another from Chiabrera, in a third from Frugoni. In the second they resemble those who, having mastered all the three styles, blend them together, and form out of them a sort of Corinthian metal compounded of various others. In like manner the Caracci used, in some of their compositions, to exhibit different styles in different figures. Thus, in the Preaching of John the Baptist, in the possession of the Certosini, (in which Crespi recognizes evident traces of Paul Veronese's manner,) Lodovico has represented the hearers of the saint in such a way, that an experienced connoisseur distinguished them by the epithets of the *Raphael*, the *Titian*, and the *Tintoretto*, in consequence of the close resemblance they bore to the respective styles of those masters. Thus also Annibale, who for some time aimed only at imitating Correggio, having at length adopted Lodovico's maxim, painted the famous altar-piece for the church of St. George; where, in the Blessed Virgin, he imitated Paul Veronese, while he took Correggio for his model in the Infant Saviour and the little St. John, Titian in the St. John the Evangelist, and Parmigianino in his truly graceful St. Catherine. In general, however, they pursued the second method; and far more numerous are the examples that might be adduced of imitations less palpable, and less constrained than the above, and so blended and modified as to produce a whole perfectly original.

What the Carracci were at first most deficient in, was the imitation of the antique, which Agostino called the "disegno di Roma." Yet he and Annibale, during their residence in that city, foreigners as they were, in some sort reproduced it, and restored it to the Romans themselves; and even Lodovico, though he remained at Bologna, on more than one occasion showed that he was not unacquainted with it. At first, observes Mengs, all three betrayed a strong predilection for Correggio, in their full contours and the general character of their design; though they did not, like him, maintain an exact equilibrium between the concave and the convex, for they chiefly affected the latter. There were some other points in which they did not strictly adhere to their model; not caring to foreshorten their heads, nor always to represent them with that smile so constantly exhibited by the Parmigianini, the Baroccis, and the Vanni. They copied their heads from nature, investing them afterwards with the charms of ideal grace. Hence Annibale's Madonnas, of which there are so many of a small size in company, display a want of original grandeur derived from his studies: the same may be said of Lodovico, who, in his more delicate heads, frequently gives us the portrait of a certain Giacomina, one of the beauties of that age. In the representation of the naked figure, the Caracci were eminently skilful; and it would be doing them a manifest wrong to suppose they did not entertain a high opinion of Buonarruoti, when they imitated in this respect; though one of them once observed, not without some bitterness of feeling toward the Roman school, that Michael Angelo should have put a little more flesh upon the bones of his figures, as their own Tibaldi had done. Of such naked figures they availed themselves in their compositions more sparingly than the Florentines, though not so sparingly as the painters of other schools. In their dresses they did not so much affect curious minuteness, or the richness visible in Paul Veronese's, as a degree of naturalness in the folds and the cut of the drapery; nor did any school display mantles of a more ample size, or disposed them with more dignity around their figures.

Notwithstanding that they had studied the works of the Lombard and Venetian painters, Mengs denies that they were eminent as colourists; and this opinion is corroborated by various oil paintings (especially Lodovico's) now faded and almost defaced. This arose either from the defective nature of the grounds, or from the excessive use of oil, or else because sufficient time was not allowed to intervene between the preparation of the grounds and the execution of the picture. The same remark does not apply to their frescos. These, when viewed near at hand, display a boldness of pencilling almost equal to that of Paul Veronese's; nor, according to Bellori, did either the Carracci themselves, or any other artist of that age, produce a better-coloured work than their paintings in the Casa Magnani. There is in these a truth, a force, a blending, and harmony of colouring, sufficient to entitle them to the name of reformers even in this branch of the art. They banished those yellow and languid tints which cupidity had introduced instead of the azures and other colours of a higher price.

In action and expression they were fond of vivacity, but never sought it at the expense of decorum, of which they were strictly observant; indeed, there was not a single grace of art which they would not have sacrificed to this. Their taste in invention and composition approaches pretty closely to that of Raphael. The Carracci were by no means lavish of their figures; with the exception of such as represented popular assemblies or battle-pieces, they deemed twelve a sufficient number for any historical subject; and even in these they introduced them with moderation, in order that the different groups might produce the more effect. That they knew how to compose with judgment, correct keeping, and variety, is evident from various altar-pieces of theirs which treat of sacred subjects; in which they did their utmost to avoid the hacknied representation of a Madonna attended by various Saints. Still more evident is this in their pictures from profane story; and in none more so than in those of Romulus in the palace just mentioned. Here the three cousins display a sort of universality in painting: at once evincing their skill in perspective, landscape painting, decoration, and in every branch of art, they here combine, as it were in one point of view, every kind of excellence that we can wish for in a single work. Nor do they appear to be three different painters, but one only; a circumstance that may be remarked also in several of the collections and many of the churches in Bologna. They held, indeed, the same maxims, and in that studio of theirs prepared their designs, conferred together upon their merits, and finished their pictures, in concert. With regard to certain altar-pieces, it is still a matter of doubt whether we should refer them to Annibale or to Lodovico; and the three historical pieces from the New Testament, at the Sampieri palace, where the three relatives took it into their hands to emulate each other, do not betray such a degree of diversity as might serve to characterize their respective authors. There have been those who have remarked that, in general, Lodovico made nearer approaches to Titian's manner than did his relatives, while Agostino showed a greater predilection for Tintoretto, Annibale for Coreggio. Others have been of opinion, that the first affected a greater degree of lightness in his figures, the third a greater degree of fulness, while the second held a middle course between them. At Bologna, I found the preference was given to Lodovico for grandeur, to Agostino for invention, and to Annibale for gracefulness of style. On these points I leave it to every one to form his own opinion according to his own opportunities; and now proceed to consider the artists themselves individually.

LODOVICO CARRACCI.

Lodovico has left us specimens of the sublimest style in many of his performances at Bologna. That *Predica* of his, so admirable both for the architectural ornaments and the design of the figures; that St. Jerome who, with pen in hand, raises his eyes to heaven with an air of so much gravity and dignity; that Limbo of Holy Fathers, which, as if for the purpose of renewing his delight in it, he repeated at the cathedral of Piacenza, and sketched under a Crucifixion at Ferrara,—have, in this school, ever been considered as models of the sublime. Nevertheless, on examining the Assumption at the Teresani, the Paradise at the Barnabiti, or the St. George, in which we meet with that admirable representation of a virgin, who, struck with terror, betakes herself to flight; you will probably be of opinion that Annibale himself could not have diffused more gracefulness over the figures of maidens and boys. Lodovico's talent, therefore, was not confined to mere grandeur of style; he excelled in every department; and it would even seem that he was anxious to assert his claim to this merit in the two frescos (now no longer in existence) with which he decorated the Lambertini chapel in the church of St. Dominic. In one of these frescos he portrayed that holy founder of the Dominican order, together with St. Francis, in a manner wholly easy and unconstrained in appearance, with few lights and few shades, but those of a strongly marked character, with few folds in the drapery, and heads expressive of the highest sanctity; and this picture, according to Malvasia, proved to be "of a grandeur that has never been surpassed." In the other he gave a representation of Charity, in so soft, finished, and graceful a style, that, says his biographer, it was ever afterwards looked up to as "a model and pattern in ancient painting." He goes on to observe, that Albani, Guido, and Domenichino derived their sweetness of style from this picture; just as, in all probability, Guercino derived his first style from the St. Dominic, and Annibale his strong chiaroscuro from the St. Paul at the Convertiti. In a word, if we may credit history, Lodovico is to his school what Homer was among the Greeks, the *fons ingeniorum*. All the others have found in him that which constituted their own characteristic manner, and this because he was profoundly skilled in every department of art.

As a fresco painter, he appears to most advantage in the cloister of S. Michele in Bosco, where, in conjunction with his scholars, he represented the actions of St. Benedict and St. Cecilia, in thirty-seven pieces of different sizes. The Fire at Monte Cassino, and some few other pieces, are by his own hand; the rest is the work of Guido, Tiarini, Massari, Cavedone, Spada, Garbieri, Brizzi, and others of his youthful followers; paintings that have since been engraved, and such as are worthy of the reformers of that age. At sight of this gallery, as it might be called, of pictures produced by different artists, one might almost bestow on Lodovico's school this trite panegyric;—that from it, as from the Trojan horse, there issued forth none but princes. But what does him still greater honour is, that his cousins looked up to him to the very last as a preceptor; insomuch that Annibale, on completing the paintings of the Farnese ceiling, invited him to Rome in order that he might have the benefit of his opinion, advice, and final directions with regard to that great work. At Rome he remained less than a fortnight, and, returning to his favourite Bologna, survived Agostino seventeen, and Annibale ten years. Thus bereaved of his cousins, and advanced in years, he executed his works in a less studied, indeed, but still a masterly manner. Nor ought some few inaccuracies of design, into which he fell about this time, to detract from his fame; as in the hand of the Saviour, for instance, who is in the act of bidding St. Matthew follow him; or in the foot of the Virgin, in the Annunciation painted for the church of S. Pietro,—an error which he did not discover till it was too late, and his grief for which may be said to have caused his death.

AGOSTINO CARRACCI.

Agostino painted but little, being occupied for the most part in engraving, which not only afforded him a livelihood, but supplied him also with the means of making a figure among artists. In this painting sustained a severe loss, deprived of a genius no less calculated than that of his relatives to promote the progress of art. He possessed greater power of invention than either of the other Carracci: many, too, consider him superior to the others in design; and it is certain that in his engravings he amended and improved upon the contours of the originals. On his return from Venice he applied himself more successfully to colouring; and succeeded so well in a painting which he executed of a horse, as to deceive a real living one, — a circumstance which procured Apelles so much applause. He became a candidate in competition with Annibale, for an altarpiece proposed to be painted at the Certosini. The preference was given to his design; and then it was that, in his Communion of St Jerome, he produced one of the most celebrated pictures of Bologna. It would seem impossible to add any thing to the devotion of the aged Saint, to the piety of the Priest who administers the sacrament to him, or to the expression of the bystanders who sustain the dying man, who listen to his last words, and, that they may not forget them, commit them to paper on the spot,—countenances full of variety and vivacity, and each of them marked with appropriate mind. No sooner was the picture exhibited to view, than their pupils thronged around it to make their designs; insomuch that Annibale, moved with jealousy, began, like his brother, to take more time and pains; endeavouring at the same time to turn Agostino's attention once more to the art of engraving: a scheme in which he succeeded. At Rome, however, he had to contend with him again as a painter; and the beautiful poetical imagery so much admired in the paintings of the Farnese ceiling, is in great part the offspring of his genius, to which indeed we are indebted for the stories of Cefalus and Galatea; those charming performances, that one might fancy to have been dictated by a poet, and executed by a Greek artist. It was noised about at the time, that, in the pictures of the Farnese palace, the engraver surpassed the painter; so that Annibale, no longer able to endure the stings of envy, under feigned pretences dismissed his brother from the work; nor could either the humility of Agostino, the advice of his elders, or the mediation of the great, suffice to appease him.

Quitting Rome, therefore, Agostino entered the service of the Duke of Parma, in one of the saloons of whose palace he painted Celestial, Terrestrial, and Venal Love; a most beautiful performance, which he executed only just before his death. One figure still remained to be added; and this the Duke would never suffer to be supplied by any other hand. On finding the end of his days draw near, he was seized with the deepest remorse for his lascivious engravings, and bitterly lamented having published them. At the same time, too, he designed a picture of the Last Judgment, which, however, he was unable to complete. In the description of his funeral, and in the oration recited on that occasion by Lucio Faberio, mention is made of an unfinished head of Christ, in the character of the universal judge, which was painted by him at that time on a black ground. This head is now shown in the Albani palace at Rome, and a duplicate of it may be seen elsewhere: in those features we find exhibited, at one view, all that the human mind can conceive of the majestic and the terrible.

ANNIBALE CARRACCI.

Annibale distinguished himself greatly in Lombardy in every style that he chose to attempt. In his earlier works Mengs recognizes "the semblance of Coreggio's style rather than the style itself;" but it is a semblance so specious, that it forces us to acknowledge him as one of the happiest imitators of that great model. That Descent from the Cross of his, in the possession of the Capuchins of Parma, may compete with the finest works of the Parmesan school. His picture of S. Rocco,—a sort of epitome of the merits of various artists, and etched by Guido Reni—is still more celebrated. This picture, which was painted for Reggio, was afterwards removed to Modena, and from thence to Dresden. He there represented the Saint standing on a platform beside a portico, and distributing his wealth to the poor; a picture abounding in figures, but abounding yet more in instruction. A crowd of beggars of both sexes and of all ages, and labouring under every variety of infirmity, are made also to display an admirable variety in the grouping and the gestures: one takes with gratitude what is offered to him, another seems to wait with impatience, a third counts his money with exultation: all here is misery and abasement; and yet all seems to remind you of the fertility and elevation of the author's fancy. Having repaired to Rome, however, during the anno santo 1600, he entered on a new career. "He checked his ardour, (says Mengs,) dealt less in figures of an exaggerated character, and took Raphael and the ancients for his models; though, with a view to grandeur of effect, he still retained some vestiges of Coreggio's style." Albani, in a letter preserved by Bellori, makes nearly the same remark, adding that Annibale, in the opinion of the best judges, "very far surpassed his cousin, owing to having studied not only the works of Raphael, but the most beautiful of the ancient statues." He there also executed various paintings for different churches; but his happiest performances, and, as it were, the whole foundation of art as restored by him, must be looked for in the Farnese palace. The subjects were selected by Monsignor Agucchi; and, together with the allegories, may be seen described in Bellori's work. In one of the apartments were to be given "representations of the Virtues; such as the Choice of Hercules, Hercules sustaining the World, Ulysses in his character of Deliverer;" in the gallery, various stories of Virtuous Love; as those of Arion and Prometheus; and others of Vicious Love, amongst which a most stupendous bacchanal-piece, in the centre of the ceiling, is the most conspicuous. The work is admirably distributed, and varied with ovals, cornices, and Telemons, the latter sometimes in stucco, sometimes in chiaroscuro; where we recognise his continued studies on the Farnese Hercules and the Belvedere Torso, of which he could give an accurate drawing merely from memory. In the rest, too, we meet with the elegance of the ancient Greeks and the grace of Raphael, together with imitations not only of his favourite Tibaldi, but of Buonarroti also, as well as the sprightliness and strength to be found in the paintings of the Venetian and Lombard schools. This was the first work, in which, as in a Pandora's box, the various merits of all the great Italian artists were combined together in one view; and in its proper place, I noticed the sensation it created at Rome, and the revolution it occasioned in the world of art.

In consequence of this great work, Mengs assigns Annibale the next rank after the three great painters; nay, as far as regards the figures of men, he even places him before them all. In point of composition, Poussin affirmed that, next to those of Raphael, there were no works to be found surpassing these; while, to the historical pieces, admirably executed as they are, he preferred the Telamones or Termini already noticed, and the other naked figures; in which he said the painter had ever surpassed himself. Baglione ascribes to him the method of colouring from nature, which was then almost lost, as well as the natural style of landscape-painting, adopted afterwards by the Flemings. To all this we may add, his talent in caricature, which no one better knew how to copy from nature, and heighten by the powers of imagination. In the different galleries of Rome several of Annibale's pictures are to be met with in this new style of his; and of these there is one in the Lancellotti palace of a smaller size, and painted a colla, rivalling, I had almost said, the best that have been found at Herculaneum. It represents Pan teaching Apollo to play the pipe; figures designed, coloured, and arranged in a manner worthy so accomplished a master. These figures are so well managed, that in the countenance of the youthful god we read submissiveness and the fear of doing wrong; while in that of the more aged deity, who is seen looking another way, we discern attention to the performance, self-complacency at possessing such a pupil, and anxiety to conceal this feeling from him lest it should inspire him with vanity.

No works of his so exquisitely finished as those already noticed, are perhaps to be met with at Bologna; where there still exists a strong party, dating their origin from the days of the Carracci themselves, who give Lodovico the preference to Annibale. When, however, I reflect that Annibale combined with the inheritance derived from his own school the various qualities with which the great masters of ancient Greece had, in different ages and in different places, enriched their style; when, too, I reflect upon the progress made by Domenichino, Guido, Albani, and Lanfranco, on observing this new style of his at Rome; as well as the new light, which, as Passeri gives us reason to suppose, it afforded Algardi, to the great advantage of sculpture; and the improvement which, through him, took place in the delightful and attractive paintings of the Dutch and Flemish schools—the opinion commonly held beyond the limits of Bologna, that Annibale was the greatest painter of the family, appears to me to be the nearest to the truth. Let others, if they please, add, that Agostino was the greatest genius, Lodovico, to whom we are indebted for both the one and the other, the greatest master of the three.

The three Caracci may almost be said to close the period of the golden age of Italian painting. They are the last of the great masters; unless, indeed, we admit that their more distinguished pupils brought down the golden age a few years later. There arose, it is true, many eminent masters after their time; but from that period, as though they evinced less grandeur and solidity of style, we begin to meet with complaints about the decline of art. Nor have there been wanting those who have contended for an age of silver, which they date from Guido and bring down to Giordano, as well on account of the inferior merit of the artists themselves, as for the prices, (so much greater than before,) which Guido introduced. The Carracci had been but indifferently paid. Malvasia admits this, and fails not to notice the humble dwelling, and to describe the narrow circumstances in which Lodovico died: the other two died even poorer than he. For the rest, the Carracci did not, like other painters, leave any legitimate offspring to perpetuate their school: they passed their lives unfettered by matrimonial ties, and used to say that they had no wife but art. And so ardent and devoted were they in their attentions to this, that they had scarce time to think of themselves. Even while they were at table, they kept paper and pencil before them, and, whenever they observed any action or gesture worth notice, failed not to take a sketch of it on the spot.

DOMENICHINO.

Domenico Zampieri, otherwise called Domenichino, is now universally looked upon as the most distinguished scholar of the Carracci; nay, Algarotti gives him the preference even to the Carracci themselves; and, what is still more, Poussin considers him as the greatest painter next to Raphael. Passeri, in his introduction to the life of Camassei, pronounces the same opinion of him. At the commencement of his studies he appeared to be slow of understanding, and that because he was profound and accurate: indeed, Passeri ascribes his progress rather to intensity of study than brilliance of genius. By constantly acting as a censor upon himself, he became among all his fellow-students the most exact and expressive draughtsman, the best colourist, whether we consider the truth or strength of his colouring, the most universal master in the theory of art, the sole painter out of the whole number in whom Mengs could find nothing more to wish for, save a somewhat greater degree of elegance. To devote himself the more exclusively to art, he withdrew from society, or if he occasionally sought it amidst the crowds of the market-place or the theatre, it was for the purpose of observing in the countenances of the populace how nature expressed joy, anger, grief, fear, and every other emotion of the mind, in order that he might sketch them on the spot. By these means, says Bellori, he succeeded in "delineating the mind, in imparting to his works the social colouring of life," and awakening in the breast those very emotions which it is the object of each of his pictures to excite; just as a Tasso or an Ariosto would have done by the charms of his poetry. After he had pursued his studies for several years at Bologna, he repaired to Parma, to examine the beautiful works of the Lombard painters; from thence he proceeded to Rome, where he completed his education under Annibale, who also availed himself of his assistance.

His style of painting may be called dramatic; in general, he lays the scene amidst some beautiful architectural ornaments, which serve to open a way for novelty and grandeur of composition, after the manner of Paul Veronese. Here he introduces his actors, selected from nature's choicest models, and managed with the most consummate art. Those who have to play a virtuous part, have an expression so sweet, so ingenuous, and so amiable, that they can hardly fail to inspire a love of virtue. In like manner do the wicked, by their disgusting features, create in us a moral aversion to their vices. Nor let any one hope to find in the works of other painters either greater beauty or greater variety of drapery; decoration of a more graceful, or mantles of a more imposing character. The figures are disposed in such situations and such attitudes, as serve to add to the general effect; while over the whole is diffused a light that gladdens the soul, but which becomes brighter and brighter in the countenances of the more virtuous figures; whence they are the first to attract the eye and touch the heart of the spectator. The most delightful part of the spectacle is to run over the scene from one end to the other, and observe how well each personage performs the part assigned him. In general, there is no need of an interpreter to tell what is passing in the minds of the actors, or what it is that they are uttering: they all bear it stamped on their gestures and looks: were they gifted with the power of speech, they could not tell their tale to the ear more plainly than they tell it to the eye. Of this, the Flagellation of St. Andrew, in St. Gregory's at Rome, painted in competition with Guido, opposite to his St. Andrew, who is being led out to execution, is a sufficient proof. It is a common tale, that an old woman once stood a long while examining Domenichino's picture, commenting upon it part by part, and explaining it to a boy whom she happened to have with her; and that, turning afterwards to Guido's work, she took a cursory view of it, and passed on. It is added, too, that Annibale, on being made acquainted with the circumstance, was induced in consequence of it to prefer the former to the latter performance. It is further said, that Domenichino, while painting one of the executioners, sought to rouse himself to anger, using all the violence of gesticulation and language of a man in the act of denouncing threats, and that Annibale having surprised him in the fact, embraced him, and exclaimed:—"Domenichino, to-day I must take a lesson from you." So novel, and, at the same time, so just and natural did it appear to him, that the painter, like the orator, should feel within himself all that he undertakes to represent to others.

Yet this picture of the Flagellation is a mere nothing compared with the Communion of St. Jerome, or the Martyrdom of St. Agnes, or other altar-pieces which he executed at a more mature age. The first of these is generally looked upon as the best picture in Rome, next to the Transfiguration of Raphael; and the second was, by his rival, Guido, pronounced to be ten times superior to any thing of Raphael's.* In these church pictures, one great attraction consists in his glories, in which he introduces Angels of the loveliest features and the most ethereal forms, engaged in

* [illegible] Roma [illegible] p. [illegible] this decision.

the most pleasing occupations of the piece; crowning martyrs, bearing palm-branches, scattering roses, weaving the mazy dance, or making melody. In their attitudes we often trace some imitation of Coreggio's manner: their figures, however, are different, and have for the most part a peculiar comeliness which distinguishes them. But however pleasing Domenichino may be in his oil paintings, he is always more soft and harmonious in his frescos. Of these, besides those at Naples, specimens may be seen—at Fano, but the greater part of them injured by a fire; consisting of historical pieces from the New Testament, in one of the chapels of the cathedral—at the Villa Bracciano; consisting of mythological subjects—at Grotta Ferrata; consisting of the actions of S. Nilo—and at Rome; consisting of various sacred pieces scattered about in different churches. In the corbels of the cupolas of S. Carlo a' Catinari and S. Andrea della Valle, he painted, at the former, the four Cardinal Virtues, at the latter, the four Evangelists, which, after a hundred similar performances, are still looked up to as models of art. In the tribune of S. Andrea may be seen various pieces from the life of that Saint; at S. Luigi, others from the life of St. Cecilia; at St. Silvester's, on the Quirinal-hill, certain pieces from the life of David, together with other scriptural subjects, which, for the composition and the style of the drapery, are by some preferred to all the rest.

It seems almost incredible that works such as these, which now excite the admiration of professors themselves, should once have been decried to such a degree, that, for a time, their author was almost destitute of employment; and was even on the point of abandoning painting, and betaking himself to sculpture. This we may attribute partly to the arrogant assumption of his rivals, who turned his very merits into faults, partly to some little defects of his own. Domenichino excelled less in invention than in the other branches of art. Of this we have a proof in his picture of the Rosario at Bologna, which neither was then, nor is now, fully understood by the public; and it is wonderful that even his own partisans disapproved of this composition, and that the author repented of having produced it. Hence, distrusting his powers in this department, he not unfrequently borrowed from others: in his St. Jerome, he imitated Agostino; in his St. Cecilia dispensing alms, he imitated the S. Rocco of Annibale; and thus in other cases he availed himself of the ideas even of less celebrated artists; being accustomed to observe that there was no picture in which he could not find something worth copying; just as Pliny used to say there was no book from which he could not extract

[illegible]

some useful information. This tendency to imitation afforded his rivals an opportunity of taunting him with want of fancy; nay, they went so far as to get Agostino's St. Jerome engraved, and, dispersing copies of it about, denounced Zampieri as a plagiary. Lanfranco, the prime agent in these machinations, opposed, on the other hand, his own novelty of invention; contrasting his own celerity and promptness of execution with the tardiness and indecision of his rival. Had Domenichino been backed by a party proportioned to his merits, he might, like the Carracci at Bologna, have quickly triumphed over his adversaries, by showing, that though he was an imitator, he was not a servile copyist; and that if his works were of a more protracted birth, they deserved at any rate to enjoy a longer life. The public is doubtless an equitable judge; but with the public it is not always enough that our cause is good, unless we have also a powerful party to abet it. Domenichino, of a timid and retiring disposition as he was, and master of but few pupils, had not then a sufficient number on his side, and was constrained to yield to the crowd that trampled him; verifying the remark of Monsig. Agucchi, that his worth would not be rightly appreciated till after his death. Party spirit once extinguished, impartial posterity now does justice to his merits; nor is there a single royal gallery that is not ambitious of possessing specimens of his works. His figure pieces are in the very highest repute, and fetch enormous prices. They are rarely to be seen except in Capitals. His David, at the college of Fano, is an object of curiosity to all foreigners of any pretensions to taste; it is a figure as large as life, and would alone suffice to render an artist's name immortal. The St. Francis, formerly in the possession of Count Jacopo Zambeccari, of Bologna, is a small but almost inestimable picture: the Saint is represented in the act of prayer, and, from his red and bloodshot eyes, one would almost think his very heart was melting into tears. Two other pictures of his, of which the composition is singularly beautiful, did I meet with at Genoa; Venus deploring the death of Adonis, in the Durazzo gallery; and the S. Rocco offering up prayers for the cessation of a Pestilence, in the Sala Brignole. The attitude of the Saint himself—the anxiety of those who look to him for succour—the ghastly appearance of the dead extended upon the ground, more especially that of a man who is being carried to the grave, and of a mother to whose cold breast a little innocent is still seen clinging,—agitate the spectator with all the force of reality. Of Domenichino's pictures from profane story, the most celebrated is the Chase of Diana, in the Borghese palace; a picture abounding with sprightly nymphs and gay *accidents* (gai accidenti.) In the same collection, as well as in the Florentine gallery, may be seen a small landscape or two of his, and a portrait or two of his in several others. Even in these performances, too, he evinced great merit, and these are the least difficult to be procured.

ALBANI.

NEXT to Zampieri, comes his intimate friend, Francesco Albani, who, "aiming at the same end, (says Malvasia,) and adopting the same means, pursued the same glorious path." They coincided in a sort of general air of selection, solidity, and pathos, in their design: they also closely resembled each other in their colouring, except that Albani's fleshes are of a more sanguine hue, and not unfrequently impaired, owing to his method of laying on the grounds. In originality of invention he is superior to Domenichino, and perhaps to every other artist of the same school; while, in the representation of female figures, he surpasses, according to Mengs, every other painter. He is sometimes called the Anacreon of painting. As that poet acquired a high reputation by the composition of short odes, so did Albani by the composition of small pictures; and as the former constantly sings of Venuses and Cupids, of youths and maidens, so does the latter almost always make choice of the same tender and fascinating subjects for the exercise of his pencil. Nature had endowed him with a peculiar aptitude for this species of painting, his fondness for poetry increased it, and even fortune itself seemed to lead the same way; he having been blessed with a wife and twelve children of such surpassing beauty, that he had at all times the finest models for his studies before his eyes. He was master, too, of a villa most delightfully situated, where the variety of objects before him afforded him the best helps for the representation of those beautiful landscapes in which he so often indulged. Passeri awards him the highest praise even in this branch of art; observing that, while others, to adapt their figures to the landscape, or the different parts of the landscape to each other, frequently change the natural colours of objects, Albani always represented the real greens of the various trees, the transparency of water, and the serenity of the sky, in their brightest aspects, and blended them together in the sweetest harmony.

Such, in general, is the nature of the groundwork on which he places and disposes his compositions; although he occasionally introduces architectural ornaments, in which he is equally happy. His compositions frequently appear, or, to speak more correctly, re-appear, in different galleries; for he not only repeated them himself, but made his pupils take copies of them; taking care to retouch them afterwards with his own hand. Few bacchanal pieces of his are to be met with: he, in general, avoided subjects of this kind; subjects which were so admirably handled by Annibale in many of his smaller pictures, from which, if I mistake not, Albani caught the first idea of his own style; accommodating it, however, to his own genius, which was of a less manly character than Annibale's. The subjects most familiar to him were—the Sleeping Venus—the Diana in the Bath—the Danae in Bed—the Galatea in the Sea—and the Europa on the back of the Bull, a piece which may also be seen executed by him on a large scale in the Colonna and Bolognetti collections at Rome, and at Pesaro in that of the Mosca family; and it is delightful to observe those little Cupids, some of them spreading a veil over the damsel to shield her from the sun's rays, others with bands formed of flowers dragging along the bull, or goading him on with their arrows. Frequently, too, he introduces them either dancing, or weaving garlands, or practising with their bows at a heart suspended aloft for a target. Occasionally he makes painting the vehicle of some doctrine or some ingenious allegory; as in those four oval pictures of the Elements in the Borghese palace, which he afterwards repeated in the Royal gallery of Turin. In these also are seen little Cupids, some of them tempering Vulcan's darts, others spreading snares in the air for the feathered race, others fishing or disporting in the sea, others gathering flowers and weaving chaplets on the ground; as though he sought to represent the system of those among the ancients who ascribed every thing in nature to the operation of Genii, and therefore with Genii peopled the universe. Albani did not devote so much of his time to sacred subjects, nor did he depart from his usual style in them; making the entire action of them depend upon the ministration of lovely little Angels. One of the most frequently repeated of his designs is that which represents the Infant Jesus, with eyes turned towards heaven, observing the Angels, some of whom bear in their hands thorns, others scourges, or crosses, or some other emblems of his future passion. There is a picture of this kind at Florence, and it may also be seen repeated, though somewhat varied, in two beautiful altar-pieces; the one in the possession of the Dominicans of Forlì, the other in that of the Filippini of Bologna. These and other altar-pieces of Albani's, dispersed through different cities, as Matelica, Osimo, and Rimini, as well as his fresco paintings at S. Michele in Bosco at Bologna, and at S. Jacopo degli Spagnuoli, after designs of Annibale, at Rome, prove that he did not want the ability to execute large works, though he applied himself with better success and greater inclination to those on a smaller scale.

Albani kept a school of painting for many years both at Rome and Bologna, where he was the constant competitor of Guido both as a painter and a master. Hence arose the many strictures on his style, which Guido's followers affected to despise as voluptuous and effeminate, inelegant in his figures of men, and monotonous as well in his infantine figures, which always betray the same proportions, as in the heads of his Holy Families and Saints, where we always recognize the same features. These and similar charges, brought forward also against Pietro Perugino, do not serve to lower this great master in our opinion, so much as the esteem of Annibale, his own writings, and his own pupils, serve to exalt him. We read that Annibale, enraptured with a little picture of his, (where, among other things, was a fountain in which a bacchanal was pouring wine,) purchased it, and afterwards declared, that he had not even paid for those few drops of water so exquisitely coloured by the wine. Of his writings we have now only some few fragments, preserved by Mal-

vols. not very methodically arranged, it is true, (a task worthy of some other pen,) but highly valuable for the information and the precepts they contain. With regard to his pupils, Sacchi and Cignani would alone suffice to do him credit; the former of whom became one of the main supporters of the art at Rome, the other at Bologna; and owing to whose efforts, painting for several years maintained its ground in both those schools.

GUIDO.

Guido Reni is by many considered as the greatest genius of the school; nor did any other of their scholars excite the jealousy of the Caracci so much as he. Lodovico was unable to disguise it; and it was then that from a pupil he converted him into a rival, and that, to depress him, he began to take into his favour Guercino, who pursued a totally different path. Annibale himself, when, after an interval of some years, he found him his competitor at Rome, chid Albani for taking him thither; and, to lower his credit, persuaded to oppose Domenichino to him. Even so early as the age of twenty, the age at which he quitted Calvart, the Carracci discovered in him a genius no less rare than haughty and ambitious of distinction; which, at the very outset, aspired to something of the novel and the grand. In the Buonfigliuoli palace and other choice collections, there exist certain juvenile efforts of his, some in one style, some in another. He attentively studied the works of Albert Durer; imitated the Carracci; took delight in Cesi's figures; like Passerotti, aimed at imparting strong relief and accuracy to the representation of the muscles; and even made some attempts at imitating Caravaggio: in the above-mentioned palace there is a Sibyl of his, extremely beautiful in point of features, but beyond measure overcharged with shadow. Indeed, the style which he finally adopted originated solely in an observation which Annibale happened to make one day upon Caravaggio's style:—that to this method there might be opposed another of a totally different description; by introducing, instead of his partial and defective lights, others of a broader and more vivid character; by substituting the tender for the savage; the strongly marked outline for the indistinct; and transforming his low and vulgar figures into others of a more select and beautiful kind. These words made a stronger impression on Guido's mind, and rooted themselves in it more deeply, than Annibale had imagined; nor was it long before he turned his whole attention to the style thus indicated to him. Sweetness was the main object he had in view; this he aimed at in his design, his mode of pencilling, and his colouring; from that moment he began to make a free use of white lead, a colour shunned by Lodovico; and from that moment predicted the durability of his tints, a prediction verified by the event. His fellow-students became indignant at this, as though he had presumed to depart from the method of the Carracci, and return to the feeble and overrated manner of the preceding age. Nor was he wholly deaf to their advice. At first he adhered closely to that strength of style in which the Bolognese school so much delighted, attempering it, however, with more softness than is usually to be found in that school; and gradually carrying this quality to a greater length, he in a few years attained to that delicacy of manner which he had proposed to himself. Hence I have heard distinctions drawn between Guido's first and second styles, and questions raised as to which is the better of the two, more frequently at Bologna than any where else. Nor is every one disposed to bow to Malvasia's decision, who pronounced the first the most fascinating, the other the most learned.

During the progress of these changes he never lost sight of that facility which forms one of the

male attractions of the mother, and afterwards he aimed at distinguishing himself by superior beauty, especially in the graceful heads for which, in the opinion of Mengs, he surpassed every other painter, and, according to the expression of that very profound connoisseur, worthy of Paradise. In those figures Rome itself, I conceive, may envy them Bologna itself: the Fortuna of the Capitoline museum; the Aurora of the Rospigliosi pavilion; the Helen of the Spada palace; the Herodias of the Corsini collection; the Magdalen of the Barberini gallery; and other similar objects in the possession of different proprietors, are looked upon as prodigies of Guido's art. This talent for the beautiful was, according to Albani, his bitterest and constant rival, the gift of nature; it was, however, the result of his continual studies of the beauties of nature, the works of Raphael, and the statues, medallions and cameos of antiquity. He himself confessed that the Medicean Venus and Niobe were his favourite models; and rarely indeed is it that we may not recognize in his paintings either Niobe herself, or some one of her children, yet diversified in a variety of ways, and with such address, as to exempt him altogether from the charge of plagiarism. In the same manner did Guido profit by the works of Raphael, Correggio, Parmigianino, and his admired Paul Veronese; works from which he conferred to extract a thousand beauties, and that, too, in so easy and unconstrained a manner, as to move the envy even of the Carracci themselves. In fact, this artist did not so much aim at copying beautiful heads, as at forming in his own mind a sort of general and abstract idea of the beautiful, as we know to have been the case with the Greeks; and this he afterwards invested with such a character as best suited his purpose. I find it recorded, that, on being asked by one of his scholars "in qual parte del cielo, in quale idea" were to be found the models of those countenances which he portrayed, he pointed to casts of those ancient statues just alluded to, observing—you, too, may extract from these models beauties similar to those contained in my works, if you have but the genius to do it. I find, too, that he took as a model for one of his Magdalenes, the head of a colour-grinder, a head of the vulgarest character; but in Guido's hands all its defects disappeared, each feature was invested with becoming grace, and the whole became a miracle of art. He pursued the same plan in those parts of his figures exposed to view, reducing them in every instance to the most perfect forms, especially in his hands and feet, which are singularly beautiful; and the same plan he pursued in his draperies, which he not unfrequently borrowed from the engravings of Albert Durer's works, and to which, directing them of every thing like dryness, he imparted just that degree of airiness or stateliness which the subject demanded. Even his portraits, too, without altering the features of the originals, or representing them as younger than they really were, he contrived to invest with a certain air of freshness and grace; as in that of Sixtus V. in the Galli palace at Osimo; or in that stupendous one of Cardinal Spada, to be seen at Rome in the possession of his heirs. There is no action, no gesture, no emotion of the mind, which he does not contrive to portray without impairing the value of his figures; he depicts them under the varied feelings of grief, sadness, and terror, without at all detracting from their beauty; he accommodates them to every purpose, represents them under every attitude, and that without ever rendering them less pleasing: to each of them we may in some sort apply this panegyric, that in every action and in every step Beauty secretly animates and accompanies it.*

What most surprises us is, the way in which he contrives to diversify this beauty; a circumstance to be ascribed as much to the great fertility of his fancy, as to his studies. Continuing to exercise himself in design up to the latest period

* Illam, quidquid agat, quoquo vestigia vertat,
Componit furtim, subsequiturque Decor.

Tibullus.

of his life, he constantly taxed his invention how best to vary his style of beauty, that so he might exempt it from the charge of mannerism. He was fond of painting heads that looked upwards, and used to say, that he had a hundred different methods of doing this. He also varied the folds of his drapery in a hundred different ways; though he was always fond of making them ample, easy, natural, and intelligible in their origin, progress, and arrangement. Nor did he display less diversity in the mode of attiring his youthful heads, disposing them in a variety of ways, with hair sometimes dishevelled, sometimes arranged with care, at other times purposely neglected; occasionally throwing over them a veil, a handkerchief, or a turban, in a manner as novel as it was graceful. Nor did he impart less variety to the heads of old men, in which he represented, with such an air of nature, the inequality of the skin and the flow of the beard; twisting the hairs of the head in every direction, and animating the features by a few bold and vigorous touches, and by a few lights which, at a distance, produce the happiest effect; specimens of these, which are the least rare of this artist's performances, are to be seen in the Barberini and Albani galleries. He also took great pains to vary his fleshes; making them, in delicate subjects, of a pure white, and overlaying them with certain colours of a livid and azure hue mingled with middle tints; a practice which some think open to the charge of mannerism.

The panegyrics which we have just bestowed on Guido's style do not apply to all his works. His inequality is notorious; and this inequality is attributable, not to his system, but to a vice which in some measure obscured his many virtues—his love of play. His earnings might have been a fortune to him; and yet, in consequence of his losses, he was continually in want; and his wants he supplied by executing his works in a careless manner. Hence some few errors in perspective, and some few defects in invention; faults dwelt upon with so much aggravation by the implacable Albani: hence, too, the incorrectness of his design, and the inequality between his different figures, as well as the habit of setting his works to sale before he had finished them. Not that they are therefore excluded even from royal collections: in that of Turin, there is a Marsyas most exquisitely finished, before whom stands an Apollo little better than a mere daub. To form a proper estimate of Guido's merits, however, we must turn our eyes to those other works to which he owed his fame. Among the best things of his in his boldest style, we may place—the Crucifixion of St. Peter at Rome—the Miracle of the Manna, at Ravenna—the Conception, at Forli—the Massacre of the Innocents, at Bologna—and the celebrated picture of St. Peter and St. Paul, at the Casa

Sangiorgi in the same town. In his other manner, we may more particularly notice—the St. Michael, at Rome—the Purification, at Modena—the S. Giobbe, at Bologna—the St. Thomas the Apostle, at Pesaro—and the Assumption, at Genoa, one of the most studied of Guido's works, and placed opposite the St. Ignatius of Rubens.

Guido opened a school of painting at Rome, as well as in his native place, where, as we learn from Crespi, he reckoned more than two hundred scholars among his followers. Nor, however, that we are, by this number, to estimate his dignity as a teacher. He was in truth a master, who introduced into the works of every school a still softer and sweeter style, which in the time of Malvasia was called the modern style. His very rivals profited by it; for it is held to be a matter of certainty, that Domenichino, Albani, Lanfranco, and their more distinguished scholars, were indebted to Guido for that tenderness in which they sometimes surpass the Caracci themselves. He did not let his scholars begin by copying his own works; exercising them at first in those of Lodovico and others of the earlier masters. Crespi is moreover of opinion, that he grounded his scholars in the true principles of art, of imitation, and of the other more important matters, without wasting their time over those minutiae which are easily enough learnt in the course of practice.

GUERCINO.

Giovanni Francesco Barbieri, surnamed Il Guercino da Cento, might, to speak the plain truth, more properly be placed among the painters of Ferrara, of which city Cento is a dependency, than among those of Bologna: but we must follow the more common practice, and rank him among the Caracceschi. This practice originated either in a tradition that, while a boy, he received some lessons from the Caracci in the art of design; a tradition which but ill accords with the period at which he lived; or else, because he received a hint for painting from an altar-piece of Lodovico's; which is but a very slight ground for reckoning him among that artist's scholars. For the rest, he never attended the school of the Caracci; but having resided a short time at Bologna with Cremonini, his fellow-countryman, he returned to Cento; where he became at first the scholar, next the colleague, and lastly the kinsman of the elder Benedetto Gennari. There are those who reckon among Guercino's masters one Gio. Batista Gennari, who, in 1606, painted at S. Biagio of Bologna a Madonna amongst various Saints, in a style very much resembling that of the Procaccini. To say the truth, too, the Paradise at S. Spirito di Cento, as well as an altar-piece at the Capuchins, and others of the earlier works of Guercino, betray vestiges of the manner of the old masters. He afterwards, in conjunction with Benedetto, directed all his efforts to impart to his pictures an imposing effect: in his endeavours after which, I shall not, with the generality of biographers and dilettanti, content myself with distinguishing two styles only, he having avowedly professed three; as Righetti, in his Description of the Pictures of Cento, also observes.

Of these, the first is the least known: it abounds with very strong shadows interspersed with vivid lights, is but little studied in the heads and the extremities, while, in point of colouring, the fleshes are of a yellowish tinge, and the other parts not of a very agreeable character; a manner which on the whole bears some faint resemblance to that of Caravaggio: specimens of it are to be seen not only at Cento, but at Bologna in the S. Guglielmo a' Ministri degli Infermi. From this he passed on to his second manner, which is the most esteemed and the most sought after. This he went on improving for the space of several years by means of the helps he derived from various other schools; having, during this period, frequently visited Bologna, spent some time at Venice, resided a Feyears at Rome, in company with the more eminent of the Caravaggisti, and also contracted an intimacy with Caravaggio. This his second style is invariably founded on that of Caravaggio; displaying strong contrast of light and shade, both of them of the boldest character; yet including great sweetness in the blending, and consummate art in the relief; a quality so highly prized in this profession. Hence foreigners have sometimes denominated him the magician of Italian painting; and by him we have seen renewed those celebrated illusions of antiquity; such as that of a child reaching out its hand in stealth to snatch some fruit that he had painted. From Caravaggio also he borrowed that indistinctness of outline, of which he availed himself to execute his pictures with the more despatch; he imitated him also in those half-length figures placed in one and the same plane; nay, for the most part he composed his historical pieces in that manner. He aimed, however, at greater chasteness of design and greater selection than Caravaggio; not that he ever attained to a certain elegance and dignity of feature; but he represented, in general, heads worthy of a judicious observer of nature; displaying a gracefulness of air, an ease and truth of attitude, and a colouring which, if it is not the most delicate, is at least the most sound and juicy. Frequently, on comparing Guido's figures with Guercino's, we should feel disposed to say, in the words of one of the ancients, that the former had fed on roses, the latter on flesh. To know how admirably he succeeded in the colouring of his draperies after the manner of the more distinguished Venetians, as well as in the colouring of his landscapes and accessories, we have only to look at his S. Petronilla in the Quirinal palace, or the Resurrection of Christ at Cento, or his S. Helena in the possession of the Mendicants at Venice; all of them admirable pictures in his second style. In this style also are most of his works that are still to be found at Rome, not excepting even those on a larger scale; as the S. Gio. Grisogono on the ceiling of the church of that name, or the Aurora of the Villa Ludovisi. But he eclipsed both these and all his other performances in the cupola of the cathedral of Piacenza, in which city he seems to have wrought in competition with Pordenone, and in boldness (fierezza) of style to have surpassed him.

Some years after his return from Rome to Cento, observing how much people in general were taken with the sweetness of Guido's manner, he resolved to emulate it; thenceforward departing gradually more and more from the robust manner hitherto described, and painting in a gayer and more open style. He also imparted a greater degree of comeliness and variety to his heads, and became more studious of expression; a point carried to a more astonishing pitch in several of his pictures executed about this time. There are some who date this change of style from the period of Guido's death, when Guercino, finding that he could now take the lead at Bologna, quitted Cento and established himself in that great city. Several pictures, however, in his third manner, executed previous to Reni's death, compel us to reject this supposition: nay, it is even said that Guido observed the change, and turned it into a cause of self-congratulation; declaring that, while he did his utmost to keep aloof from Guercino's style, the latter did all he could to approach his. In this style, though modified by the preceding, is the Circumcision of our Saviour placed in the church of Gesu e Maria at Bologna; a piece in which the architectural ornaments and the drapery vie with the figures, while, with regard to the latter, it is hard to say whether they charm us more by their proportions or their expression. To this we may add, the Espousals of the Virgin at S. Paterniano of Fano, the S. Palazia at Ancona, the Annunciation at Forli, and the Prodigal Son in the royal palace at Turin; a piece which consists of full-length figures, and of which duplicates, in half-length figures, may be seen in many different galleries. However pleasing this his third manner may be found, competent judges could have been well content had Guercino never departed from the vigour of his second style, for which nature had peculiarly adapted him, and in which he may be considered as unique. The number of orders he received may perhaps have contributed to make him hit upon an easier method, as well as his incredible talent for execution and despatch; he having produced no less than one hundred and six altar-pieces, and one hundred and forty-four large cabinet pictures for princes and persons of distinction, to say nothing of numberless others which he painted for private individuals; such as Madonnas, portraits, half-length figures, and little landscapes. Hence his works are by no means rare in the different collections. The Zolli family at Rimini possesses about twenty pieces of his; the Lecchi family of Brescia also possesses a large number, all of them admirable and highly finished according to his usual practice: among the latter is a portrait of a Frate Osservante, his confessor —a prodigy of art.

LANFRANCO.

Giovanni Lanfranco, one of those distinguished disciples of the Carracci who followed Annibale to Rome, was born at Parma, and, while a youth, was in the service of the Conti Scotti of Placentia; where, having in mere sport designed some figures in charcoal upon a wall, his rare genius was discovered; and, in order that it might be cultivated, he himself was placed under the care of Agostino Carracci. Bellori, quaintly perhaps, but still with some degree of truth, sought to describe the nature of his genius by his name; and it must be confessed, that it would not be easy to find a painter of a character more *frank* either in conception or execution. He hit upon a sort of style which, in design and expression, bears some resemblance to that of the Carracci, while in composition it approaches that of Coreggio; a style at once easy and grand, whether we regard the dignity of the heads and the attitudes, the broad and well distributed masses of light and shade, or the stateliness of the drapery, disposed in broad imposing folds hitherto unknown in art. It is to this very circumstance of its grandeur, that we must impute the want of attention to those minutiae which add to the value of other paintings as much as they would have detracted from his. In this style, therefore, it was very possible for him to be somewhat careless of exact finish, and to succeed in pleasing notwithstanding; possessing, as he did, so many other qualities to excite our admiration;—novel inventions; colours, if not lively, yet exquisitely blended together; foreshortenings the most beautiful; together with a mode of contrasting the different figures and the different parts of his pictures, which, as Mengs observes, has served as a model for the tasteful style of more modern artists.

This method of his he adopted in very many cabinet pictures, not only for the Farnese princes, in whose palace at Rome he executed some of his earliest works, but for other persons of distinction. Among those that gained him the greatest applause in that city is his Polyphemus, painted for the Borghese gallery, and his scriptural pieces at S. Calisto. His altar-pieces, too, are very numerous; and among the best may be reckoned—the S. Andrea Avellino, at Rome, set off with stately architectural ornaments—the Dead Christ, at Fuligno, with the Eternal Father, who, though clothed in a mortal shape, inspires us nevertheless with awful ideas of the Divine Being—the Death of the Virgin, at Macerata—and the S. Rocco and the S. Corrado, at Placentia; pictures which may perhaps be ranked among the most finished and the most renowned of all that Lanfranco ever produced. But more especially did he employ this method in his cupolas and other similar works which he executed on a large scale after the manner of Coreggio. While a youth, he had prepared at Parma a small coloured model of the cupola of the cathedral, emulating its style in every part, especially in gracefulness of movement (grazia delle movenze), the most difficult of all. This he imitated in the church of S. Andrea della Valle at Rome; following in his paintings there the example which M. Angelo had set in architecture, when finding it impossible to create a more beautiful cupola than that of Brunelleschi, and unwilling to make one like it, he formed one after a different plan, and yet succeeded to admiration. This work at S. Andrea della Valle forms a sort of epoch in the art, inasmuch as Lanfranco, to use the words of Passeri, "fu il primo a dilucidare l' apertura di una gloria celeste con la viva espressione di un immenso luminoso splendore, senza esserne per l' innanzi veduto esempio." "The cupola of Lanfranco (he continues) remains an unrivalled example in the way of glories: for, as far as we can form any idea of these glories, he has, in the opinion of the most dispassionate judges, attained the highest pitch of excellence, not only in the general harmony of the whole, which is the main point, but in the distribution of the colours, the arrangement of the parts, and the strong character of the chiaroscuro," &c. Nor was this work, on which he spent four years, the only proof he gave of a fertility and elevation of fancy altogether unexampled even among the painters of antiquity. The cupolas which he painted in Naples at the church of the Jesuits and in the treasury of St. Januarius, where he succeeded Domenichino, together with the different tribunes and chapels which he decorated in the same masterly manner in both the above-mentioned cities, have, in this kind, furnished Lower Italy with the most assured models it ever possessed. From him the machinists learnt the true art of contenting the eye at great distances; painting only a portion of the picture, and, as he was wont to say, leaving the air to paint the rest (dipingendo in parte, e in parte, come egli soleva dire, lasciando che l' aria ci dipinga).*

* [illegible], Andrea Camassei, [illegible], Alessandro [illegible], [illegible], [illegible], [illegible]dore, and Luca [illegible], etc. Of some only the [illegible] and who were all of them [illegible] are less commonly omitted. Of the [illegible] which is [illegible]

omitted, the principal ornaments are Pasinelli and Cignani: the former of these aimed at combining Raphael's design with the attractions of Paolo Veronese's style; the latter, Coreggio's grace with Annibale's profound knowledge of the art.

THE END

LONDON:

IBOTSON AND PALMER, PRINTERS, SAVOY STREET, STRAND.

Printed in the United States
125009LV00003BA/1/A

9 780548 161821